Cambridge Elements

Elements in Eighteenth-Century Connections
edited by
Eve Tavor Bannet
*University of Oklahoma*
Markman Ellis
*Queen Mary University of London*

# EARLY ENGLISH PERIODICALS AND EARLY MODERN SOCIAL MEDIA

Margaret J. M. Ezell
*Texas A&M University*

Shaftesbury Road, Cambridge CB2 8EA, United Kingdom

One Liberty Plaza, 20th Floor, New York, NY 10006, USA

477 Williamstown Road, Port Melbourne, VIC 3207, Australia

314–321, 3rd Floor, Plot 3, Splendor Forum, Jasola District Centre, New Delhi – 110025, India

103 Penang Road, #05–06/07, Visioncrest Commercial, Singapore 238467

Cambridge University Press is part of Cambridge University Press & Assessment, a department of the University of Cambridge.

We share the University's mission to contribute to society through the pursuit of education, learning and research at the highest international levels of excellence.

www.cambridge.org
Information on this title: www.cambridge.org/9781009507240

DOI: 10.1017/9781108866590



First published 2024

*A catalogue record for this publication is available from the British Library.*

ISBN 978-1-009-50724-0 Hardback
ISBN 978-1-108-79174-8 Paperback
ISSN 2632-5578 (online)
ISSN 2632-556X (print)

# Early English Periodicals and Early Modern Social Media

Elements in Eighteenth-Century Connections

DOI: 10.1017/9781108866590
First published online: May 2024

---

Margaret J. M. Ezell
*Texas A&M University*

**Author for correspondence:** Margaret J.M. Ezell, m-ezell@tamu.edu

**Abstract:** Using the lens of early modern social authorship and contemporary social media, this Element explores a new print genre popular in England at the end of the seventeenth and early eighteenth centuries, the periodical. Traditionally, literary history has focused on only one aspect, the periodical essay. This Element returns the periodical to its original, complex literary ecosystem as an ephemeral text competing for an emerging audience, growing out of a social authorship culture. It argues that the relationship between authors, publishers, and audiences in the early periodicals is a dynamic participatory culture, similar to what modern readers encounter in the early phases of the transition from print to digital, as seen in social media. Like our current evolving digital environment, the periodical also experienced a shift from its original practices stressing sociability to a more commercially driven media ecology. This title is also available as Open Access on Cambridge Core.

**Keywords:** social authorship, periodicals, social media, participatory cultures, print culture



ISBNs: 9781009507240 (HB), 9781108791748 (PB), 9781108866590 (OC)
ISSNs: 2632-5578 (online), 2632-556X (print)

# Contents

# 1 Introduction: Early English Periodicals and Early Modern Social Media Forms

> Social authors take advantage of the interactive elements afforded by Web 2.0 infrastructures to form an online community. . . . These authors' online connection to their audience is not driven by their royalty publisher, but by their own choice to expand the author – reader dynamic.
>
> R. Lyle Skains, *Digital Authorship: Publishing in the Attention Economy* (2019)

> What can one learn from [this] early culture of authorship that is relevant to our current situation? Are we returning to the early modern model of manuscript text and social authorship?
>
> Margaret J. M. Ezell, *Social Authorship and the Advent of Print* (1999)[1]

In 1999, I concluded my study of a feature of late seventeenth- and early eighteenth-century literary culture, social authorship, by wondering what, if any, application that model might have for the emerging digital publication media at the turn of the twentieth century. I argued then that English literary culture in the early modern period was marked by a vibrant literary culture based on the circulation of handwritten, manuscript copies, which complemented and competed with a burgeoning print market for the attention of writers and readers. In this model of coterie or social authorship, readers were also writers, editors, and curators of their own and their coterie's literary productions, not merely passive, paying consumers of it. This is not the same as "scribal publication," where professional scribes reproduced handwritten manuscript texts that were commissioned or purchased by readers, often clandestinely; instead, social authorship, as its name implies, values interactive, reciprocal forms of literary exchange with no financial aim, a form of literary culture that we now know continued well into the late eighteenth and early nineteenth centuries.[2]

In this brief study, I would like to apply this concept of social authorship to explore, paradoxically, a highly commercial form of print media which became popular in England at the end of the seventeenth and early eighteenth centuries, the periodical. In particular, I will look at how in its early stages, periodicals made use of the practices found in the older social manuscript literary cultures to attract and sustain a paying readership. Questions quickly suggest themselves when we observe how this genre changed over time: How did an originally cheap form of printed ephemera become a collectible literary commodity, with some of its

[1] Skains, *Digital Authorship*, pp. 54–55.

[2] For studies of scribal authorship, see Hobbs, Marotti, Woudhuysen, and Love; for examples from eighteenth century and later of the continuation of social authorship in the context of print culture, see Schellenberg, Levy, and McKitterick.

authors such as Joseph Addison, Richard Steele, and Samuel Johnson, joining the ranks of canonical English writers? What were the expectations of the original periodical readers of the genre as compared to today's academic ones? Why do many of the strategies and tactics employed by early periodical writers and publishers to create and sustain an audience seem so familiar to us now, during a transition period from commercial print to digital media?

Those familiar with early modern authorship practices in general, including social authorship and scribal publication, find themselves surprised by the enthusiasm which the commentators on digital media have typically declared that the shift from paper to screen, from print to digital, is a "revolutionary" phenomenon, creating a new forms of literacy, journalism, and of course, literary culture – as the nerdy genius Egon in the film *Ghostbusters* announced in 1984, "print is dead," and it is commonplace to assert that "no one" now reads except on a screen.[3] While indeed the digital media ecology is transforming the traditional print one as found in the twentieth century, is it as original and unprecedented in its practices, as is often declared?

This is not intended as an in-depth scholarly comparison between early eighteenth-century print and twenty, twenty-first digital media, but instead an experiment to see what emerges when one thinks about the practices and issues for writers and readers of each, what might a juxtaposition of observations about the ecology or behavior of each might cause us to see occurring in the other. Rather than only looking for transhistorical parallels, by using the lens of digital authorship practices in the age of contemporary social media, we may also disrupt in a positive way traditional formulations of eighteenth-century periodical writing, which would then permit us to see aspects of past practices usually overlooked. Referencing features of participatory culture in the digital age, I hope, highlights those within late seventeenth- and early eighteenth-century literary ecologies which permitted and propelled the popularity of those periodicals while shaping their contents. Observing the nature of the dynamics of earlier periods' literary ecologies may well also serve as a gentle corrective to the often-ahistorical understanding of our own literary ecology that is manifest in discussions of digital authorship practices. Finally, we see in the changes between practices found in the early periodicals such the *Gentleman's Journal* and those in the *Rambler* a different type of relationship between readers and authors, which, while gesturing at the expected formal elements established in the earlier periodicals, rejected the dynamics of participatory literary culture for creating content.

[3] See for example, Jeff Gomez, *Print Is Dead: Books in Our Digital Age* (2007); for a more nuanced account of media shifts and social changes, see Bolter, *The Digital Plenitude* (2019), and on the "myth of the disappearing media," Ballatore and Natale, "E-readers and the death of the book" (2016).

Most twentieth- and twenty-first-century readers who are familiar with the early periodicals I will explore know them through the classroom and know only a tiny fraction of the writers who were engaged in creating them. One thing that clearly emerges is that in our modern teaching anthologies and in most critical discussions of the origins of periodicals, the entries under the names Addison and Steele consist only of a portion of the original contents of the *Spectator* or *Tatler*. Typically, only the essay in each issue is offered to modern readers, with no mention of the other contents that characterized the periodical form, the flower cut off, as it were, from a complex literary ecosystem. Modern readers are presented with short pithy essays conveniently packaged as examples of timeless, enduring English "literature" that serve as exemplary English prose models: in fact, in their complete and complex original publication format, the *Tattler* and the *Spectator* were ephemeral publications that were competing for readership in an aggressively expanding "new" media market. Likewise, grouping Samuel Johnson with Addison and Steele as the masters of the periodical essay based on the essays' contents and narrative voices obscures not only what these authors shared as writers for periodical publications, but also the ways in which Johnson chose to deliberately reject many of the conventions that his predecessors had used so successfully, signaling a significant change in the nature of the periodical genre in the process.

## 1.1 General Characteristics of Early English Periodicals

*British Newspapers and Periodicals 1641–1700: Short Title Catalogue* (1987) broadly defines periodicals from this period as being "numbered and/ or dated issues of proposed or actual sequences of pamphlets or sheets, bearing uniform titles and formats."[4] It has been estimated that approximately "one-quarter of the publications in Britain between 1641 and 1700 were issues of serials (or 'periodicals' in British usage)," offering multiple formats for readers to choose from: "over 700 such titles were published, including newsbooks, newspapers, literary and leisure miscellanies, trade bulletins and official journals."[5] Although as we shall see, subsequent commentators have assigned this new genre significant cultural weight, it was originally an ephemeral product. It is important to realize that the term "periodical," according to the *Oxford English Dictionary*, did not come into widespread usage until the latter part of the eighteenth century to signify "a magazine or journal issued at regular or stated intervals (usually weekly, monthly, or quarterly)." Seventeenth- and eighteenth-century readers and writers, however, generally referred to them simply as "papers."

[4] *British Newspapers and Periodicals 1641–1700: A Short Title Catalogue*, p. vii.

[5] *BNP*, p. vii.

As the editors of a recent collection of essays on women's periodicals in the eighteenth century have noted, "periodical" "is a deeply difficult term to define in the eighteenth-century context: It can reasonably be argued to encompass everything from the news-sheet, to the advice column, to the essay periodical, or the magazine or even pseudo-periodicals."[6] They characterize periodicals in the long eighteenth century as being comprised of "hundreds of titles, many short-lived and hard to trace; others stunningly voluminous and hard to summarize." They urge that rather than attempt to divide these ephemeral publications into discreet subgenres, such as newspapers versus literary periodicals versus magazines, the periodical should be understood in an eighteenth-century context: that "periodical culture" was composed of "diverse but contiguous" forms. I would suggest that this is not unlike our evolving digital media culture, as My Space competed with Facebook, and YouTube spawned TikTok.

That said, some general characteristics can be cautiously suggested when one is speaking of the type of early eighteenth-century periodical publications, which have been enshrined within traditional literary histories and classroom anthologies. These periodicals typically appeared weekly, if not more often – the *Tatler*, for example, was published three days a week and the *Spectator* initially appeared daily – and they appeared on specific days announced in the publication. They were typically printed either with two columns, front and back, on a single folio half sheet, as were the *Athenian Mercury* and the *Spectator*, or as a small quarto pamphlet, such as Daniel Defoe used for the *Review*. They were relatively inexpensive publications: It is estimated that the *Spectator* cost two pence each issue, but it is also the case that many people enjoyed reading them for free, courtesy of their favorite coffee house which often offered a wide array of ephemeral printed materials for the entertainment of their customers. They were not intended to be primarily a private reading experience but, as Abigail Williams has suggested about eighteenth-century reading practices in general, a shared one, whether reading aloud in the family or listening to others in public spaces.[7]

## 1.2 English Periodicals in Literary History

The names "Addison and Steele," like Shakespeare's contemporaries Beaumont and Fletcher, are inevitably coupled in literary histories. Together, these two friends and collaborators, Joseph Addison and Richard Steele, and the essays they published in the periodicals the *Tatler* and the *Spector* helped create later generations' perceptions of both the early eighteenth-century culture in which

---

[6] Batchelor and Powell, *Women's Periodicals and Print Culture in Britain, 1690–1820s*, p. 8.

[7] Williams, *The Social Life of Books*.

they lived, and the genre in which the wrote, the periodical essay. In essays of around 2,500 words, they presented their views on contemporary topics ranging from the silliness of Italian opera and contemporary women's hair styles to the poetics of Milton's *Paradise Lost* and the importance of commerce and the merchant class in England.

The eighteenth-century periodical essay has long been considered by literary critics to be a new English literary genre that, like the novel, arose out of rapidly changing social structures in the early eighteenth century. Its contents have been typically described as providing a particularly good window into the manners and tastes of its original readers. In addition, canonical authors have been seen as helping to shape those tastes, acting as powerful social influencers, Terry Eagleton, echoing a nineteenth-century biographer's observation that Addison was the "chief architect of Public Opinion in the eighteenth century," endorses the essential point that the *Spectator* determined the topics and attitudes of "this ceaseless circulation of polite discourse among rational subjects . . . the cementing of a new power bloc at the level of the sign."[8]

In terms of genre, the periodical essay has enjoyed lasting critical approval. Samuel Johnson, himself the leading critical voice at the end of the eighteenth century, proclaimed Addison's essays as being models of English prose style that addressed subjects of universal truth and human nature. Of course, not all readers agreed with this assessment: The narrator in Jane Austen's *Northanger Abbey* (1818), defended young ladies reading novels by Frances Burney as opposed to the more socially acceptable *Spectator*, noting that "either the matter or manner" would "disgust a young person of taste . . . their language, too, frequently so coarse as to give no very favorable idea of the age that could endure it."[9] On the other hand, nineteenth-century academic commentators such as Henry Reed (1808–1854), the first American editor of William Wordsworth, applauded the ways in which Steele and Addison had turned away from the "grossness of manners and speech which had disgraced society in the years just previously . . . the mire of that obscenity which defiled the times of Charles the Second."[10]

In the early twentieth century, the admiration for Addison and Steele continued. Walter Graham in his history of the English periodical press enthused that while there had been periodicals published in the seventeenth century, it was "produced by inferior pens," and that from the beginning of the eighteenth century, "the periodical was the nursery of literary genius."[11] The online Virginia Open Anthology of Literature in English created in the twenty-first

[8] Eagleton, *The Function of Criticism*, pp. 13–14.

[9] Austen, *Northanger Abbey,* p. 24.

[10] Reed, *Lectures on English Literatures*, p. 230.

[11] Graham, *English Literary Periodicals*, p. 13.

century, declares that the *Spectator* "set the pattern for a kind of essay writing that persists to the present day. . . . written in a clear and straightforward style without partisanship or professional jargon: This is a mode that is still standard in print and online journalism."[12] In his provocatively entitled 1990 work *Addison and Steele Are Dead: The English Department, Its Canon, and the Professionalization of Literary Criticism*, Brian McCrea argues that it is exactly these qualities of clarity and inclusiveness in the essays' accommodation for a "mass" audience which caused Addison and Steele to lessen in popularity in academic literary circles in the 1970s and 1980s, in favor of the more arcane and thus more in need of scholarly interpretation works by Swift and Sterne.[13]

For much of the twentieth century, however, the vehicle for these essays, the eighteenth-century periodical publication itself, was a dead zone for most literary scholars. This was in part due to the difficulties in studying the original ephemeral publications prior to the creation of digital databases, but principally because with the exception of the ones written by these literary geniuses – Defoe, Addison, and Steele – periodicals were considered to be "subliterature" and not worth the effort to read.[14] By the mid-1970s, there were some literary historians who began to find the periodical itself as a genre of more interest; James Tierney pointed out that "curious indeed is a situation where many who have made the eighteenth century their life's study have never examined more than a pittance of what the contemporary British was actually reading."[15] In particular, the *Spectator* again became significant, not this time for its elegant prose style, but as part of the mechanism Jürgen Habermas argued it helped to create, a "bourgeois public sphere" through the cultivation of public opinion and the formation of good taste.[16] Commentators such as Timothy Dykstal and Erin Mackie subsequently pointed to the ways in which the contents of popular periodicals such as the *Spectator* and the *Tatler* chronicle a society transitioning into a bourgeois, capitalist society whose increasing urban middleclass readership had a seemingly insatiable desire for fashionable consumer products, especially those produced from England's expanding colonial spaces.[17] In the 1980s, the bold claim was made that historians viewed periodicals as "an important source of insight into the early development of modern society in the West."[18] As J. A. Downie noted in the late 1980s, for "the ideological critic, the periodical essay can truly be said to be a happy hunting ground."[19]

---

[12] "The *Spectator*," https://virginia-anthology.org/the-spectator/.

[13] See McCrea, *Addison and Steele Are Dead.* [14] Tierney, "British Periodicals," p. 168.

[15] Tierney, "British Periodicals," p. 167.

[16] Cowan, "Mr. Spectator and the Coffeehouse Public Sphere."

[17] See Dykstal, "The Politics of Taste in the 'Spectator'" and Mackie, *Market a la Mode.*

[18] Botein, "The Periodical Press in Eighteenth-Century English and French Society," p. 464.

[19] Downie, "Reflections on the Origins of the Periodical Essay," p. 302.

Presently, when we read or teach eighteenth-century periodical essays in our classrooms, regardless of whether we consider them to be exemplars of English prose style or windows into eighteenth-century English culture, we encounter them first as important literary texts worthy of being enshrined in internationally sold anthologies for the teaching of English literature. The tenth edition of one of the most widely used classroom anthologies, *The Norton*, offers twenty-six pages in a section on the *Tatler* and the *Spectator* and eleven pages of the section on Samuel Johnson are given to the *Rambler* and the *Idler*: Addison and Steele are credited as developing "one of the most characteristic types of eighteenth-century literature, the periodical essay."[20] The *Norton* likewise offers students "the grave *Rambler* essays, which established his reputation as a stylist and a moralist . . . what Johson uniquely offers us is the quality of his understanding of the human condition" (711, 712). Broadview Press's *Anthology* includes as well as these authors some excerpts from the *Female Tatler* and the *Female Spectator*, and describes the periodical essay as being an important step in the development of commercial print culture that "played a prominent role in the formation of popular taste and political opinion."[21]

In the anthologies' presentation of the periodical as a genre, care is given to make an attribution of individual essays, either to Steele or Addison, or more rarely the occasional contribution by a friend, such as the poet Alexander Pope or Lady Mary Wortley Montagu. Attention is also focused on the use of fictional first-person narrators, Isaac Bickerstaff and Mr. Spectator, as a characteristic feature of eighteenth-century satire. Samuel Johnson is represented as attaining the pinnacle of the genre but there is very little sense of the *Rambler* and the *Idler* as having originally been written for ephemeral publications, and in the case of the *Idler*, surrounded by other materials. By stripping the essays out from their material context, this trio of neatly packaged early periodical authors has worked well as part of a chronological anthology to represent popular eighteenth-century taste and manners as well as the development of the essay as a significant literary genre alongside the novel.

As interesting and important as the contents of these periodical essays are to understanding the socio-literary views of their times, as we shall see, this was not the way in which these essays were originally conceived and designed by its authors, nor received by their initial readers. When we explore the context in which Steele and then Addison were creating their periodicals, it becomes clear

[20] *The Norton Anthology of English Literature, The Restoration and the Eighteenth Century*, eds. Stephen Greenblatt, Lawrence Lipking, and James Noggle, Tenth Edition. New York: W.W. Norton, 2005, p. 461.

[21] *The Broadview Anthology of British Literature: The Restoration and the Eighteenth Century*, p. 668.

that while they were masters of the craft, they were often canny adaptors, not the inventors, of conventions from many earlier popular publications. By focusing on the content of a single element within this new genre of periodical publication, the essay, and isolating it from the context in which it was created and read, we lose the sense of the ways in which its authors engaged its original readers and the dynamic nature of this new genre, which could be interactive and multimodal.

The goal of this study is to replace the periodical essay in its original format and environment, to explore how during this formative period in the long eighteenth century, its authors and creators wove together news, entertainment, creative literary forms, and social commentary in ways not dissimilar to our contemporary digital media creators. As we shall see, early periodicals also exhibit tensions between sociability and competitive commercial strategies, which have marked the development of the internet and its media forms. We will explore how the format of the new periodicals itself draws attention to the ways in which authorship and readership were both changing in response to a developing competitive media environment, an interactive literary ecology emerging from and supported by oral, manuscript, and print practices.

In the same way that late twentieth- and early twenty-first-century readers have been migrating from older print-based technologies for writing and reading into newer internet-based digital media through what is called "remediation," seventeenth- and early eighteenth-century innovators made strategic use of "residual" features to ease that transition from one to the other. For example, still today the "save" function in Microsoft Word is the emblem of a floppy disk, a nostalgic icon of the earlier days of desktop computing of the late twentieth century, email messages on your phone can be put into an icon of a trash can, and the symbol for "search" on most digital media is an old-fashioned magnifying glass. Readers in the late seventeenth and early eighteenth century were likewise becoming accustomed to reading new forms of information and entertainment in print, and it is in earlier seventeenth-century ephemera that we find the emerging strategies for establishing an audience and maintaining readership as the media changed.

## 1.3 Creating an Audience: Topicality, Fake News, and Newsbooks

> If you're old enough to remember fax machines, you probably remember that pre-1999, we got most of our information from print media. But it's 2022 . . . Print media isn't dead, but more often than not, I believe digital media features are the way to go in 2022 and beyond.
>
> Kristen Wessel, "Should you Seek Out Online Press or Print Placements?" *Forbes*, January 25, 2022

> TikTok is fastest growing news source for UK adults . . . . A quarter of US adults say they always use TikTok to get the news, with nearly half of US millennial and Gen Z adults – under-41s and under-25s, respectively – indicating the same.
>
> Dan Milmo, *The Guardian*, July 20, 2022[22]

Readers in the second decade of the twenty-first century in search of the news are more likely than not to turn to online, digital sources and combine reading the news with watching it being performed. The transition from printed newspapers and magazines as the conveyers of both timely news and entertaining features is still ongoing, however, as many readers still are learning different ways to acquire the news information they desire, and this also requires access to the new media platforms on the internet. Those in search of news in the seventeenth century, likewise, had to learn how to acquire and to evaluate the news they sought in a volatile and rapidly changing social culture and media environment. Prior to the English Civil War, the publication of domestic "news" was illegal and controlled through a network of censorship involving the Archbishop of Canterbury, the Star Chamber, and the Stationers' Company.[23] At the start of the seventeenth century, James I had commented on what seemed to him the unseemly desire in his English subjects to find out about "the deepest mysteries that belong to the persons or state of kings and princes," with "an itching in the tongues and pens" to talk and write about these topics.[24] The government traditionally made its news known through proclamations, which were printed as broadsides, averaging 1,000 copies made by the King's printer, and then delivered to the local sheriffs by messengers to be posted in a public place in the towns.[25] The majority of the residents, however, probably learned its contents through hearing the proclamations being read aloud. Important news was also delivered orally from the pulpit: as early as the nineteenth century, the historian Thomas Babington Macaulay declared the pulpit announcements were "to a large portion of the population what the periodical press now is."[26]

There was a type of news in print which escaped the censors and was eagerly consumed by seventeenth-century English readers and their appreciative listening audiences. Along with topical ballads, pamphlets featuring "strange and terrible news" had been popular sellers since the late sixteenth century, and with the expansion of news publications in the mid-century, as Julie Sievers argues, they "played a key role in the development of the 'news'" as an emerging

[22] www.forbes.com/sites/forbescommunicationscouncil/2022/01/25/should-you-seek-out-online-press-or-print-placements/?sh=47ac43f47fb6.

[23] Raymond, *Making the News*, p. 4.

[24] Quoted in Davies, "English Political Sermons, 1603–1640," p. 2.

[25] *British Royal Proclamations Relating to America 1603–1783,* p. viii.

[26] Macaulay, *History of England from the Accession of James II,* I: 305.

concept and media form.[27] Typically, such publications featured an exciting woodcut illustration amplified by a lengthy descriptive title, such as the

> *True and Wonderful. A Discourse relating a strange and monstrous Serpent (or Dragon) lately discovered, and yet liuing, to the great annoyance and diuers slighters both of Men and Cattell, by his strong and uiolent poison, In Sussex two miles from Horsam, in a woods called S. Leonards Foreest, and thirtie miles from London, this present month of August. 1614.*

This exciting pamphlet shows a flame breathing dragon with the prostrate bodies of a man, a woman, and a cow, and a solitary dog bravely barking at it. Such "news" was presented as verifiably true, with multiple "eye and ear witnesses" willing to confirm the details, and, as seen in the dragon of Horsam, offering a high level of specific descriptive details suggesting the care taken and the veracity of the reporting.

On the other hand, strange and terrible news pamphlets also have many of the characteristics of a timeless good story: Step-mothers are merciless, murders are unnatural, and gratifyingly, the criminals typically received "most wretched endes." These ephemeral publications were designed to inform and entertain a wide audience, from those that purchased and read them to the audiences at home and in the tavern, to those who enjoyed the pictures and listening to the dramatic accounts. Such publications thus provided material for conversation for the whole group. The contents were not intended to be meditated on in private nor be carefully preserved but instead shared and circulated, making it a sociable form of print media, one speaking to immediate events and interests.

As we shall see, topicality and the use of a persuasive authorial persona found in earlier seventeenth-century pamphlets and newsbooks are characteristics of the late seventeenth- and early eighteenth-century periodicals. Not only did readers want the latest information, but they also wanted it presented with a narrative voice that generated trust in its truthfulness. As the English Civil war broke out and censorship collapsed, the pamphlet producers had a different source of shocking and sensational news of the greatest interest to their readers, but often in forms and formats familiar to the readers of strange and wonderful news. The newsbooks and pamphlets that were produced by both sides of the English Civil War in the 1640s and early 1650s loudly proclaimed the accuracy and authenticity of their content, even when it clear that the account is biased, and the narrative is serving as propaganda (Figure 1).

Between 1645 and 1660, newsbooks and pamphlets were the main source of information about domestic military and domestic events for English readers,

[27] Sievers, "Literatures of Wonder in Early Modern England and America," p. 769.

Terrible and bloudy

NEVVES

From the diſloyall Army in the

NORTH

Declaring their perfidious and tyrannicall proceedings to the whole Kingdom of *England*: As alſo the raiſing of new Forces in the Kingdome of *Scotland*, to aſſiſt *Monro* againſt Lieutenant Generall *Crumwell*. And the Lieutenant Generals *Declaration* touching the Scots. Likewiſe, a *Declaration* of the proceedings of the Levellers in *Liecester-ſhire*, under the command of Col. *Martin*, and their *Proclamation* at *Market-Harborow*. Alſo, ſtrange Newes from the Prince of *Wales*, and the Reſolution of the Souldiers in *Holland*, touching His Highneſſe.

Printed in the Yeer, 1648.

**Figure 1.** *Terrible and Bloudy Newes* (1648). (c) The British Library Board. E.462. (28).

with an estimated 300 periodical publications appearing, despite attempts by the powers in charge to control their publication through ordinances. After the censorship mechanisms collapsed during the early days of the war, with an estimate that over 300 periodical publications appeared between 1645 and 1656, although like the pamphlets few of these cheap, ephemeral publications survived.[28] They were variously referred to by titles that emphasized their speedy delivery of timely information, as well as their international scope, such as "diurnals," "gazettes," "currants," "mercuries," and "corantos," the last of which were single sheets produced in Amsterdam but printed in English which featured foreign news. While "Gazetta," is derived from Italian gossip sheets published in Venice in the mid-sixteenth century, names such as "mercurius" emphasized the importance and the veracity of the contents, being transmitted as it were by Mercury, the messenger for the classical gods.

Both forms, the pamphlet and the newsbook, were early forms of journalism that catered to the interests and literacy levels of the broadest possible audience. As one historian observed, modern readers "need not assume that the purpose of this early journalistic effort was to spread the truth. . . . Newsbooks could not help being informative," he observed, "but the truth of their content was not as important as that there be something for sale every Monday."[29] Using woodcut illustrations as well as dramatic dialogues and poetry to capture their audiences, their announced function was to inform readers and listeners of all the important political, military, and religious news of the day; they also served as political propaganda, incorporating popular ballads and sensational fictions in a witty and reader-oriented style. Sold by street vendors and "Mercury Women," who also sold ballads sheets typically for a penny, these publications like the earlier "wonders" pamphlets were also able to be enjoyed by those who heard them being read aloud in public spaces.[30]

This new print genre, however, generated anxieties that still mark readers' responses to topical media today. Since the 1930s, there has been increasing concern and anxiety in western European societies that the "news" has become merely "entertainment." However, media critics observe that "the line between news and entertainment is inherently blurred and contestable and never fully maps the boundaries between politically relevant and politically irrelevant media forms": instead, "it was only the regulations, institutions, norms, and practices that came to define the broadcast news media regime that made such distinctions seem natural."[31] Whether it is called "soft" news or, in the 2020s, "fake news," the practice of mixing entertainment with news in popular mainstream media served to keep audiences engaged and eager for more.

Marchamont Needham was a leading figure in the evolution of newsbooks. Regardless of which side he was writing for at the time, he believed in mixing

[28] Ezell, "Learning the News: Pamphlet Mercuries and Newsbooks," https://doi.org/10.1093/oso/9780191849572.001.0001.

[29] Sommerville, *The News Revolution in England*, p. 36.

[30] See Spufford, "'First Steps in Literacy."

[31] Williams and Carpini, "And That's the Way it (Was)," p. 59.

information and news with entertainment. Writing in 1649 for the royalist *Mercurius Pragmaticus*, Nedham explained the purpose of including verse in his news accounts: poetry serves "to tickle and charme the more *vulgar phant'-sie*, who little regard *Truths* in a grave and serious *garb* . . . yet I would have you know, in the midst of *jest* I am much in *earnest*."[32] In 1650, now writing for Parliament, he shows a shrewd awareness of how to amplify his voice not dissimilar to a Twitter or Instagram poster seeking to attract followers who will share his content: "The designe of this Pamphlett being to undeceive the People," he explained, "it must be written in a Jocular way, or else it will never bee cryed up."[33] Likewise, John Hall writing for Parliament in 1648 *Mercurious Britanica Alive Again* declares that the newsbook which opens with four stanzas of verse only does so because readers expect it: "thus do we according to the solemnity of a Pamphlet begin with verse; for it we should not retain the accustomed ceremonies of abusing the people, we should render them useless, and loose our labour."[34] Commenting on the audience's expectations of more than just a list of the events of the day, he makes the point that "how many Ballads would sell without a formal wood cut? These general complyances must needs to observed, or else the people out of the rate of their madnesse will not be brought to parley."

Joad Raymond has suggested that the preference for poetry as the medium for the royalists writers reached its height in *Mercurious Melancholicus* which not only featured the news in verse, but also branched out into satiric playlets with titles such as *Craftie Cromwell* (1648) and *Mistris Parliament Brought to Bed of a Monstrous Childe of Reformation* (1648).[35] Describing "poetry as integral to its identity," Raymond suggests that *Mercurious Melancholicus* from its start was a "literary" newsbook; other royalist periodicals including *Mercurious Elencticus* and *Pragmaticus* followed its lead. They, too, were formatted by opening with poems consisting of four quatrains in a ballad format to set up the contents of the editorial commentary that followed, and they proudly boast of the superiority of royalist poets and their followers.[36] In addition to reporting events, such publications also offered reflections on the state of the nation, urging royalist readers to remain loyal and encouraging those who were becoming disenchanted with Parliament to embrace their points of view.

Even with the spread of printed news with its entertaining woodcuts and verses, commercial handwritten newsletters remained competitive, offering its subscribers information such as reproducing parliamentary speeches which its printed counterparts could not. During this period, Henry Muddiman and Sir

[32] *Mercurious Pragmaticus*, April 4, 1648. [33] *Mercurious Politicus* (1650).
[34] *Mercurious Brianticus Alive Again*, May 16, 1648, p. 2
[35] See Raymond, "The Daily Muse." [36] Raymond, *The Invention of the Newspaper*, p. 165.

Joseph Williamson oversaw the production of both printed newsbooks and manuscript newsletters. As Rachael Scarborough King has noted, even though the handwritten newsletters were more expensive than a printed newsbook, costing from £5 to £20 per year as opposed to the printed pamphlet at 1*d* per issue, nevertheless the circulation of the scribal ones rivaled those of the printed versions.[37] The handwritten newsletter was a compilation of individual news items sent by letters from multiple sources, which was mailed from London to the subscriber, who was often living outside of London. These handwritten accounts were obtained by subscription and apparently enjoyed a significant readership outside the immediate environs of London.

The scribal newsletters retained residual features of private correspondence, creating an aura of exclusivity and a social connection between the reader and the imagined "author." Rather than appealing to its readers by opening with amusing verses, the handwritten versions were formatted in the form of a letter, typically opening with the salutation, "Sir," which some literary historians have compared to creating a more personal relationship with the reader, "giving the recipient the pleasant feeling that he was reading his own private correspondence."[38] We are fortunate that they were sufficiently valued by their readers that some were kept intact and collected in a set, providing invaluable information to subsequent generations of historians, and also suggesting how in the future printed ephemera might also be viewed as collectible by its readers.[39]

Whether handwritten or printed, the relationship between the creator of the newsletter or newsbook and the reader was different from that of the official proclamation, printed or announced. It is in the creation of this illusion of familiarity, of social connection, which resonates with our contemporary digital media experiences, especially in who (or what) we trust to give us news – who do we follow online? Unlike creating a news bulletin or a simple commercial, the hopeful social media influencer, for example, is advised present "content" in an attractive package, one that "gives the impression that the followers are learning more about a creator, and . . . build this relationship."[40] Essential to an influencer's success, apparently, is creating this friendly virtual relationship, cultivating the audience's sense of familiarity to create trust and loyalty. It is the prevalence of this illusion of friendship which will be explored in Section 2 "Sociable Periodicals, 1690s–1700s" on periodicals devoted primarily to

[37] R. King, "All the News that's Fit to Print," p. 103.

[38] Sutherland, *The Restoration Newspaper and Its Development*, p. 8.

[39] See, for example, The Carl H. Pforzheimer Collection of English Manuscripts at the Harry Ransom Center, University of Texas at Austin, and the 1469 manuscript newsletters sent to Sir Richard Bulstrode (1610–1711) between 1667 and 1689.

[40] "How to Build a Career as a Social Media Influencer," *The Economic Times*, November 20, 2022.

entertainment reading. In these "sociable periodicals," the reader is invited to become part of a supposedly select audience who not only support the media "platform" by acquiring all of the issues and collecting it in multiple formats, but also create much of its contents.

## 2 Sociable Periodicals, 1690s–1700s: The Royal Society of London's *Philosophical Transactions*, John Dunton's the *Athenian Mercury*, and Peter Motteux's, the *Gentleman's Journal*

> The concept of the active audience, so controversial two decades ago, is now taken for granted by everyone involved in and around the media industry.
>
> –Henry Jenkins, *Fans, Bloggers, and Gamers: Exploring Participatory Culture*[41]

After the restoration of the monarchy in 1660, writers and publishers were eager to satisfy the expanding reading public's appetite for topical news combined with entertainment, a combination to which readers had become accustomed through the popular mid-century newsbooks and pamphlets. Continuing many of the practices established by those earlier periodicals, these new publications also shared several formal characteristics that helped to establish a bond with their readers: For example, they typically featured a standard title page format that was dated, with numbered issues and volumes, and which contained information about the regular publishing days during the week and from whence the publications could be obtained and advertising left. These features highlight that the contents were part of an ongoing narrative sequence, a serial publication rather than a single title. In contrast to purchasing an individual sensational pamphlet, these serial publications, although ephemeral in nature, sought to engage their readers' attentions over the long term, and to build a stable, loyal readership for that particular title. Much like modern media marketing, the periodicals employed various strategies to encourage and entice their readers to look forward to each new issue and other literary "products" associated with that title. In addition, these new style periodicals encouraged the active participation of their readers, to create content for the periodical for the pleasure of the association rather than any financial or business inducement.

### 2.1 Publishing Serial Periodicals and Topical News

The serial nature of these publications was both a challenge for the writers and publishers and a marketing advantage. It challenged the booksellers to produce their periodicals on schedule, with informative, entertaining content. On the other hand, it enabled the publishers to point readers to content in previous

[41] Jenkins, *Fans, Bloggers, and Gamers*, p. 1

issues, an interactive feature that relied on the reader to have been engaged with the periodical over a span of time and to be willing to reread this supposedly disposable ephemeral work. It also creates the conditions under which the reader can anticipate the paper being worth while holding on to over time and rereading. To promote that feature, as we will see with the bookseller John Dunton, single sheet publications could be packaged later as collected bound volumes, with extra features such as indexes and companion volumes – and the ephemeral is transformed into the collectible.

Book historians grappling with the large question of what is "print culture" and how can it be recognized have pointed to this element of seriality as being a central factor in making the claim that such a culture existed. "There is a strong argument to be made," Jason McElligott and Eve Patten suggest, "that it is impossible to conceive of a print culture in any society without the presence of serial publication: *corantoes*, newsbooks, newspapers, magazines, or literary journals."[42] Serial publications not only demonstrate that the technical ability existed to produce texts reliably in a fixed pattern of publication but they also extended booksellers' ability to attract buyers on a regular, predictable schedule: "The development of seriality was obviously a function of living in interesting times," they observe, "but it was also a striking technical achievement and a sophisticated commercial strategy" (6). As we shall see, it also created new avenues for sales, both through including advertisements and what today we would refer to as "spin-off" merchandising, or just "merch."

What I am referring to in this section as "sociable" periodicals had a different style of relationship with their readers, in contrast to that of the also newly forming genre of the newspaper. For example, during this period, the *London Gazette* stakes its claim to be the oldest continuously printed newspaper in Britain. It first appeared under the title the *Oxford Gazette* on November 7, 1665 when the court had relocated to Oxford attempting to escape the Great Plague decimating London. On the court's return, it was rechristened the *London Gazette* on February 5, 1666, with the seasoned journalist Henry Muddiman overseeing its publication until 1688.[43] During this time, Muddiman also continued his very successful manuscript subscription newsletter, mentioned in the previous section, which had the advantage of being able to report on parliamentary proceedings, which was once again forbidden to appear in printed accounts. Initially published as a single sheet with two columns on each side, *London Gazette* subscribers were assured every issue that its contents were "Published by Authority."

42 McElligott and Patten, *New Directions in Book History*, p. 5.
43 See Muddiman, *The King's Journalist*.

The contents of the *Gazette* were derived from multiple sources both international and domestic. Readers of the February 5, 1665 issue learned from a dispatch from Falmouth dated January 27 that a ship of eighty tons from Dublin filled with tallow and hides, bound for Cadiz, "proves so leaky" that the Captain was obliged to cut short the voyage and sell the goods and the ship itself. From Rome, we read an account dated January 16 of how the Pope fearing that Christendom is rushing into war asked the Cardinals to join with him to pray that war would be avoided. The account of this pious action is combined with gossip that the French representative to the Vatican had been strongly offended by the performance there by "a company of Ordinary Players" of a play which he viewed as mocking the French and he had "complained to the Popes [*sic*] Nephew of this designed insolence and National dishounour."[44] The *Gazette*, like the manuscript newsletters that had proceeded them, was dependent on the steady flow of letters from a network of business and diplomatic correspondence for its contents.

## 2.2 The Royal Society and the Philosophical Transactions

While the *London Gazette* became established as the source of reliable, government authorized information about shipping, diplomatic events, and military matters, other contemporary periodicals focused elsewhere. Through the publication of its *Philosophical Transactions* starting in 1665, the newly formed Royal Society of London kept its members informed of scientific developments in London and the provinces, on the continent, and in the Americas. Its full title gives some sense of its original scope and appeal: *Philosophical Transactions: Giving some Accompt of the Present Undertakings, Studies and Labours of the Ingenious in Many Considerable Parts of the World*.

Initially, its contents reflected the scientific interests and international connections of the first secretary of the Royal Society, Henry Oldenburg. Oldenburg had informed the eminent scientist Robert Boyle that he intended to establish a manuscript subscription newsletter devoted to science, but perhaps in response to the appearance of the French print periodical, the *Journal des Scavans,* he instead developed a monthly printed publication which sold for a shilling a copy.[45] Oldenburg was the compiler, editor, and also a contributor. In the "Introduction" to the first issue, he explains that "there is nothing more necessary for promoting the improvements of Philosophical Matters, than the communicating to such as apply their Studies and Endeavours that way, such

[44] www.thegazette.co.uk/London/issue/24/page/1.

[45] The origins of the *Philosophical Transactions* are well-documented: For a brief account, see the "Royal Society of London *Philosophical Transactions*: 350 Years of Publishing at the Royal Society 1665–2015."

things as are discovered or put in practice by others"; he concluded that "it is therefore thought fit to employ the *Press*," as the best means of sharing discoveries both in England and in "other parts of the World."[46]

The table of contents of this first issue reflects the wide range of topics to be found inside and the ways in which content came to Oldenburg: "A Spot in one of the Belts of Jupiter," was the discovery of Robert Hook, who did "some months since, intimate to a friend of his, that he had, with an excellent twelve foot Telescope, observed, some days before, he than [*sic*] spoke of it (*videl.* On the nineth of *May*, 1664, about 9 of the clock at night) a small Spot on the biggest of the 3 obscure *Belts* of *Jupiter*."[47] A lengthy synopsis of a publication from France followed, sent by its author, the French astronomer Adrian Auzout, on the motion of a recent comet. This was followed by a list of experiments being conducted by Robert Boyle; Boyle additionally communicated news of "a very odd Monstrous Calf," communicated to him in a letter from Mr. David Thomas from Hampshire.[48] Finally, an anonymous "understanding and hardy Sea-man," had contributed an eye-witness account of whale fishing in the West Indies. Clearly, the journal offered something for every interest remotely connected to the new mode of science, very broadly defined. There is no indication that any of the contributors received or expected payment.

For the rest of the seventeenth century and the first half of the eighteenth, the contents of *The Philosophical Transactions* were determined the editor alone, who was typically the Secretary of the Society. By 1693 when John Dunton's the *Athenian Mercury*, was well established, Richard Waller had the editorship of the *Transactions*. Issue 196 contained a posthumous account of Boyle's method for making Phosphorus, an exchange in Latin by John Wallis, extracts of two letters from the continental scientist Anthonie van Leeuwenhoek to Dr. Gale, Waller's own description and anatomical drawings based on his dissection of a rat, and a list of books recently published. This practice of including a medley of topics and accounts at the discretion of the Secretary alone lasted until 1752, when the financial side of the periodical was taken over by the Society itself and the process for submitting materials became regularized, with a committee of twenty-one Society members formed to decide what merited publication.

## 2.3 John Dunton, the Athenian Mercury, and the Ladies Mercury

By the 1690s, other periodicals began to appear that offered the general reader the chance to engage with a variety of topics ranging from theology to astronomy and

46 *The Philosophical Transactions*, Vol. 1, n. 1, p. 1 The early issues are available for free at www.jstor.org/stable/101400.

47 *Philosophical Transactions*, Vol. I, 1: 3.

48 *Philosophical Transactions*, Vol. 1, 1: 10.

literary pursuits. The publisher and bookseller John Dunton previously was known to Restoration scholars primarily as a struggling, quarrelsome bookseller who published his autobiography, *The Life and Errors of John Dunton* (1705). In the last few decades, however, he has become increasingly studied for his successful development of the "question-answer" periodical, the *Athenian Mercury*, and in particular his attempts to engage women readers, resulting in the *Ladies' Mercury* (1693).[49] Helen Berry has made a compelling case for the *Athenian Mercury* as "one of the most original and culturally-significant works to have emerged from the popular press" in the late Stuart period, indeed the forerunner of "what we would now recognize as an embryonic mass media" (6). In addition, E. J. Clery views Dunton as "the greatest early innovator of the discourse of feminization."[50]

Dunton's success and his impact with this journal came from an original idea to generate content for his paper: While manuscript newsletters had encouraged readers also to be correspondents and to contribute information to be circulated, Dunton invited "All Persons whosoever" to send "any Questions that their own Satisfaction or curiosity shall prompt 'em to," and, as long as the questions were not malicious, obscene, or promoting atheism, they would be answered by a sociable club of anonymous intellectuals. In his autobiography, he recorded how the idea for this new type of periodical came to him as he was walking home one evening, a publication whose content relied on questions on an astonishing range of topics submitted by its readers. Dunton attributes the inspiration to the Bible, Acts 17.21: "For all the Athenians and strangers which were there spent their time in nothing else, but either to tell, or to hear some new thing." The title of the periodical was originally the *Athenian Gazette*, which highlighted its claims to veracity and topicality. However, Dunton records in his memoir that "to oblige Authority," the title was changed to the *Athenian Mercury*; it is also possible that Dunton perhaps realized this association with the government was a limitation on the potential of the journal rather than an asset.

The design, as laid out in the first issue, was ambitious by any standard. It was supposed

> to satisfy all *ingenious and curious Enquirers* into *Speculations,* Divine, Moral and Natural, &c and to remove those Difficulties and Dissatisfactions, that shame or fear of appearing ridiculous by asking Questions, may cause several Persons to labour under, who now have opportunities of being *resolv'd* in any Question without knowing their Informer.[51]

[49] See Berry, *Gender, Society, and Print Culture in Late Stuart England.*

[50] Clery, "*The Feminization Debate,*" p. 26.

[51] *Athenian Mercury*, issue #1, March 17, 1691.

Because Dunton had imagined the periodical to be the platform for a type of learned society or club, whose interests encompassed "the whole compass of Learning," and because it was to appear twice weekly, as Dunton noted, it "required dispatch" in assembling his experts.[52] "The Athenian Society had their first meeting in my brain," he confesses.[53] To answer the questions posed, he initially called on for help from his associate the mathematician and schoolmaster Richard Sault; it would appear that in launching the new project that Dunton and Sault composed both the questions and the answers for the first two issues. Questions in these initial issues, which presumably would inspire readers to submit their own for future ones, included "whether the Torments of the damn'd are visible to the Saints in Heaven? & vice versa," "Whether 'tis lawful for a Man to beat this Wife?" "What is the Cause of Dreams?" and "Why does the Needle in the Sea Compass always turn to the North?" After the first few issues, the ingenious Mr. Sault was joined by Dunton's brother-in-law the Reverend Samuel Wesley (an Anglican minister and poet and the father of the future founders of Methodism, John and Charles Wesley), and occasionally by "Dr. Norris," identified variously as either the physician Edward Norris, or Dr. John Norris, the poet and philosopher associated with the Cambridge Platonist.[54]

Berry and Shevelow have interpreted the readership of the *Athenian Mercury* once it was established as being composed of the "middling sort" of reader; commenting on the frontispiece in Charles Gildon's *History of the Athenian Society* (1692; Figure 2), Berry notes that illustration, "the most striking aspect is its social diversity and inclusion of men and women of all ranks presenting questions to the Athenian Society."[55] It is significant to note that in addition to the "Athenians" being anonymous experts, the readers who submitted questions also retained their anonymity, each question being presented as a numbered query. As Dunton noted, this protected the reader from being revealed as either poorly educated or being young and naïve; it also gave license to ask about a seemingly unlimited range of topics.

The success of the *Athenian Mercury* was clearly its format and the use of a new method of textual transmission to create content. Instead of relying on government dispatches or shipping accounts for its contents, the *Athenian Mercury* instead relied upon its readers to suggest questions by sending them in letters to Dunton in London through the newly established Penny Post. The Advertisement at the end of the first issue reiterates how readers can become involved with this ingenious design to promote human knowledge.

52 Dunton, *Life and Errors*, I: 189. 53 Dunton, *Life and Errors*, I: 188.
54 Berry, "Dunton, John (1659–1732), bookseller." *ODNB*.
55 Berry, *Gender, Society, and Print Culture*, p. 64; Shevelow, *Women and Print* Culture, pp. 82–86.

**Figure 2.** *Emblem of the Athenian Society* (1692). © The Trustees of the British Museum.

> All Persons whosoever may be resolved gratis in any Questions that their own Satisfaction or curiosity shall prompt 'em to, if they send their Questions [in] a Penny Post letter to Mr. Smith at his Coffee-house at Stocks-Market in the Poultry, where orders are given for the reception of such Letters, and care shall be taken for their Resolution by the next weekly paper.

Writing in hindsight about the early response to the call for questions from readers, Dunton records that "the Project being surprising and unthought of, we were immediately overloaded with Letters; and sometimes I have found several hundreds for me at Mr. Smith's Coffee-house in Stocks Market, where we usually met to consult matters."[56]

The Penny Post had been established in 1680 by William Dockwra and taken over by the government in 1682; by the time of the *Athenian Mercury* in the early 1690s, it would have been a well-established and familiar mode of communication.[57] This new form of textual technology made London publishers and booksellers such as Dunton accessible to a wide range of readers outside London proper; as the invitation to "all people" suggests, individuals such as genteel young ladies who might never enter a London coffee house to read the papers or present their writings in person now had an inexpensive way of accessing the London publishing market and the booksellers had an apparently unlimited supply of free content makers.[58]

Indeed, so many women readers responded enthusiastically to the new format and publishing venue that for four weeks in spring of 1693, Dunton produced the spin-off, the *Ladies Mercury* separately.[59] The first issue opens with an address "To the Athenians," assuring the gentlemen that "*Your Worth and* Learning *to which we must pay a just* Esteem, *is the occasion of this* Address, *in which we desire you to excuse this* Undertaking, *as not at all intended to encbroach* [*sic*] *upon your* Athenian Province."[60] Continuing in a deferential strain, the presumably female speaker promises that the "fair and larger Field; the Examination of Learning, Nature, Arts, Sciences, and indeed the whole World" will remain a masculine province while "*We are for sitting down with* Martha's *humbler part, a little homely* Cookery, *the dishing up a small Treat of* Love, &c."

56 Dunton, *Life and Errors*, I: 189.

57 See Brumell, *The Local Posts of London, 1680–1840* (1938); T. Todd, *William Dockwra and the Rest of the Undertakers* (1952).

58 See Ezell, "Late Seventeenth-Century Women Writers and the Penny Post" and Berry, *Gender, Society, and Print Culture in Late Stuart England*, pp. 56–57.

59 Available online through Adam Matthews Digital. "Eighteenth Century Journals." https://www.18thcjournals.amdigital.co.uk/; and "Defining Gender." https://www.amdigital.co.uk/collection/defining-gender.

60 *Ladies Mercury*, I: 1 (February 28, 1693/94).

In contrast to the regular issues of the *Athenian Mercury*, where the questions are presented merely as numbered queries, those featured in the *Ladies Mercury* contextualize the question with information about the situation of the writer. This narration results in much longer questions and also much more complicated answers that offer advice as much as information. It also supports the voice of a sophisticated female responder, or rather the corporate voice of a "female society," which appears not to be shocked by even the most complex emotional entanglements and potentially compromising situations.

The very first question, for example, is posed by a "very young woman," who had the misfortune to be seduced by "a lewd and infamous Trifler, with whom I secretly continued this vile and unhappy Conversation for near a Twelve Month together." Her dilemma, however, is not how to negotiate her way out of social ruin from this premartial affair but how to assuage her guilty conscience when she enters into marriage with "the kindest and most passionate of men," who is besotted with her and she with him: "The more I dote on him, and he the like on me, a rueful Remembrance makes me consider my self so much the more unworthy of him." She declares that she is "haunted" by "what Delusion and Pollution I brought to his Bed; what practiced Cheats and Impostures have I used, all my affected feigned Innocence . . . practiced even the vilest of Arts in his very Bridal Night Joys, being in that dearest Scene the highest of Counterfeits." The Answer urges her to put her sin against Heaven behind her and "when that Honourable Lover afterwards addres'd himself, no Obligation even of the most Rigid Laws compel'd you to be your own Accuser," and it was not up to her to point out his mistake in believing her a virgin. As "your sin lyes concealed from the world," no "infamy" is attached to their union, and pragmatically, she should "exert thy tenderest, kindest, duteous, softest Love in all the opening, blooming, ravishing, melting fragrance, that the whole Paradise of Truth and Faith, with all its endless boundless Joys can give him," and keep her repentance to herself.

As the Advertisement made at the end of the first number makes clear, both "Ladies and Gentlemen" are asked to send their questions to "the Latin-Coffee House in Ave-Mary Lane." The second question in the first issue comes from a young man, not quite of age yet, who is making "honourable Love to a young and Beautiful Lady." He describes in some detail the nature of this wooing and its "Innocent Dalliances," which involve passionate, reciprocal kisses and embraces, firing his imaginings of "the Raptures of Possession." His concern is whether such thoughts and acts are sinful, although he hopes that being "a Good Christian and a Good Lover are things not incompatible." This query required only a brief assurance that if a marriage followed, no sin was involved.

The second issue published Sunday a week later on March 6, appears to have built upon the favorable response to the first, for its advertisement announces that questions on love are still being solicited and that the third issue will be published on the following Friday. It noted that "the Ladies Society" sought to provide answers "with all the Zeal and Softness becoming the Sex."[61] The *Ladies Mercury*, in fact, had only four issues, but were highly influential in shaping imitators seeking to enter this entertaining new market, which offered the reader a combination of scandal and probity, romantic scenarios, and supposedly a peek behind the curtains of respectability of one's fellow readers, familiar today in personal advice columns.[62] Although the advice column is typically described as an invention of mid-nineteenth-century newspaper proprietors, the argument has also been made that it was a feature of eighteenth-century American periodicals as well. Lisa Logan points to the popularity of the "Dear Matron" column which appeared in the Boston periodical *The Gentleman and Lady's Town and Country Magazine: or, Repository of Instruction and Entertainment* (1784–1785) which features questions about topics such as bigamy and adultery answered by the "worldly-wise wit of a respected (and respectable) woman."[63] This desire, however, to have advice as well as to preserve one's anonymity, tracks neatly from Dunton in the previous century through current periodicals.

In addition to devoting individual issues to questions posed and supposedly answered by women, Dunton also began offering special issues featuring verse. In a December issue in 1691, a reader wondered "Is there ever a Poet among the Athenian Society, and supposed a Question shou'd be sent in Verse, shou'd it be anser'd in the same?"[64] The journal had published individual poems prior to this, but in January 1692/93 the first "poetical mercury" appeared. As Barbara Benedict has noted over the latter part of the seventeenth and beginning of the eighteenth centuries, "periodicals thus became a new venue for publication by part-time writers, amateur critics, and authors in training."[65] The young Jonathan Swift, writing from his position as Secretary to Sir William Temple in 1691 sent his "Ode to the Athenian Society," perhaps his first published poem, to Dunton, asking if it could be printed in the supplement of the Fifth Volume, observing that "since every Body pretends to trouble you with their Follies, I thought I might claim the Priviledge [*sic*] of an English-man, and put in my share among the rest," and that "before its seeing the World, I submit it

[61] *Ladies Mercury*, I: 2 (March 6, 1693/94).

[62] See Nicola Parsons, "The *Ladies Mercury*," and Slaney Chadwick Ross, "John Dunton's *Ladies Mercury*" for analyses of ladies as readers and as subjects to be regulated.

[63] Logan, "'Dear Matron,'" p. 57. [64] *Athenian Mercury*, December 1, 1691.

[65] Benedict, "Publishing and Reading Poetry," p. 76.

wholly to the Correction of your Pens."[66] Temple, Dunton notes in his *Life and Errors*, was "a man of clear judgment and wonderful penetration" and "pleased to honour me with frequent Letters and questions, very curious and uncommon," while he characterizes Swift only as "a Country Gentleman."[67]

Perhaps the most celebrated poet who contributed to the *Athenian Mercury* was the young Elizabeth Singer Rowe (1674–1737), not long out of boarding school. Rowe would go on to achieve literary fame during her lifetime for her poetry and her prose fiction.[68] The young woman had by 1694 become, in Katheryn King's words, "the leading contributor of verse to the *Mercury*." King speculates that she had begun in 1691 by sending "poetically inclined" queries; her first known poem was printed October 21, 1693, "Habbakkuk," which even though it was introduced as being "somewhat uncorrect," was nevertheless published "for the Honour of her Sex" – the Athenians responded enthusiastically in the poem which followed it, "How *vast* a *Genius sparkles* in each *Line*!"[69] The full poem later appeared in Rowe's *Poems on Several Occasions Written by Philomela* (1696), which was also published by Dunton, who crowned her "the Pindarick Lady." Heidi Lauden suggests that following her contributions to the *Athenian Mercury*, one can "see how she consciously carves out a space for herself in the public domain and craft, with the help of the Athenians, a poetic identity that becomes a critical component to the periodical and to her own future success."[70]

There is no evidence that Dunton offered payment to those readers such as Swift and Rowe who contributed to the content of the *Athenian Mercury*, nor indeed that they expected any. There is no doubt, however, that the periodical was a successful commercial venture for Dunton. The Athenian publications were remarkably popular for many years, typically appearing in single sheets twice weekly between March 1691 and 1697 (Figure 3). Such was their appeal, Dunton also collected the individual papers and bound them into volumes, each composed of thirty issues, which Dunton records "swelled at least to Twenty Volumes folio" and which, like the single sheets, could be purchased at his shop. As his biographer Gilbert McEwen noted, such was his confidence in the sales

66 Temple, "To the Athenian Society," *Supplement to Volume 5* (1691), p. 76; As critics have observed, this Ode was modelled after Abraham Cowley's "Ode to the Royal Society"; Daniel Cook argues that it is not a failed attempt at panegyric but instead a satire. See Cook, "Swift after Cowley" and Moyra Haslett, "Swift and Conversational Culture."

67 Dunton, *Life and Errors*, I: 193.

68 See Backscheider, *Elizabeth Singer Rowe and the Development of the English Novel* for a critical reassessment of her literary stature.

69 *Athenian Mercury*: 11, no. 30 (December 1, 1693); King, "Elizabeth Singer Rowe's Tactical Use of Print and Manuscript," p. 163.

70 Lauden, "Birthing the Poet," p. 8.

Vol. 5. Numb. 4.

# The Athenian Mercury:

Saturday, *December* 12. 1691.

Queſt. 1. A*S within this week I was travelling between* Kenford, *and Bury* St. *Edmonds, I was unfortunately ſet on by three Men* in Diſguiſe, *who not finding their expected Booty, were ſo incenſed as to rifle me of all my Cloaths, and were ſending me home naked, had not one good-natur'd, and more compaſſionate Rogue than the reſt told his* Brothers in Iniquity, (pulling the Evangeliſts out of his pocket) *That if the Gentleman wou'd ſwear to ſend them 5 Guinea's to ſuch a houſe, and promiſe upon Oath not to diſcover them, I ſhou'd enjoy my Cloaths, otherwiſe I muſt expect to be ill treated, and expoſed to the Weather: So I ſwallowed their Oath, willing to be at liberty, and ſound, promiſing all; but before I pay the Money, I have a Mind to know your Opinion, Whether the Oath be Obligatory, I'm ſatisfied almoſt about it; and if the publick good by bringing theſe* Road-plagues *to Juſtice wou'd not be ſatisfactory for the breach thereof: Give me a Solution by the middle of this Month, for this Money is to be paid ſpeedily?*

*Anſw.* An Oath is not properly ſo, unleſs it be *free* and *unconfin'd*; Fear, Paſſion, *&c.* which are the Cauſes of an Oath ought to be *repented* of as ſuch, rather than the Oath it ſelf, which by the by will ſhow the *unſincerity of Death-bed Repentances.* But to anſwer the Queſtion directly, we are ſatisfied that the Queriſt is not only *free from his Oath*, it being forc'd from him, but he is alſo oblig'd to uſe what lawful means he can to ſecure the intended *Receiver of the Money*, if not the reſt that are concerned, thô *Honour, Good-nature,* &c. may tempt him to the contrary.—— Our Reaſon is this, We are commanded by God to obey the Magiſtrate, but the Magiſtrate has eſtabliſh'd ſuch and ſuch Laws, which not only contradict, but puniſh ſuch practices: Therefore whoever is acceſſary, (as the Queriſt is if he keeps his Oath) acts contradiſtinctly to the *Laws of God, and the Laws of Nations.* Our Advice is this, That the Queriſt repent of the Raſhneſs, Ignorance, and Cowardize of ſuch an Oath, and that he reſolve for the future to *ſuffer bravely in any juſt and honourable* Cauſe, rather than oppoſe Truth and Juſtice for little baſe ends. We cou'd give ſeveral other Reaſons that his Oath is cancell'd, if the Caſe was as doubtful as formerly, but every Caſuiſt is now ſatisfied. Read Mr. *Perkins Caſes of Conſcience*, ch. 13. p. 230.

Queſt. 2. *What Language was ſpoken by our Firſt Parents in Paradiſe?*

*Anſw.* The *Britiſh* wou'd perſwade us 'twas theirs, and the *Iriſh* ſure will put in too for the Honour, ſince their Chronicles, they'll tell you, run up almoſt as high, and they are ſure there was a Schoolmaſter of their Nation, who taught the *Iriſh* Grammar in the *plain of Shinar*, ſo early did they begin to be *Learned.* But leaſt ſome ſhou'd be ſo uncivil to queſtion their Memoirs being authentick, wee'll e'ne let 'em alone to ſtand by themſelves, and impoſe nothing on the Reader. That Wag *Hudibras* puts in for the *German*, when he mentions Mother *Eve*, and *the Serpents tempting her — By an High-Dutch interpreter*; which Fancy he founded as the Notes tell us, on a Fancy of *Garopius Becanus*, who takes a great deal of pains to prove the *High-Dutch*, which was his own, the Primitive Language. But rejecting all theſe, as hardly carrying the Face of probability, we think the *Hebrew*, or *Sacred Language* ſtands much fairer for't than any others; for all the Names we find mention'd in Hiſtory of the beginning of the World were undoubtedly *Hebrew.* None we think who believe the Scriptures, can queſtion that *Adam* was really the Name of the firſt Man, and *Eve* of the firſt Woman, or that theſe Names are *Hebrew*, the word *Adam*, ſignifying much more than Red or Ruddy, for which we generally take it, namely, a florid whiteneſs, and the brightneſs and luſtre proper to Pearls and precious Stones; *Eve*, a Mother, as the Scripture tells us, *Iſſa*, which *Adam* firſt call'd his Wife when he ſaw her, *Vira*, or a *She woman.* But this is alſo very remarkable in the Hebrew Names of all living Creatures, impos'd by *Adam*, which appear not to be given by chance, or deflected from any other *Language*, as the *Greek, Latin*, and all others, but to contain therein the Nature of the Creature, as the Learned and Induſtrious *Bochart* admirably proves in his *Hierozoicon*, where he ſhows that their *Names* were partly taken from ſomething obvious to the Senſes, as their Colour, their Hair, their Stature, and external form; partly from their inward properties and diſpoſitions, which he cou'd neither know by uſe, nor the Information of others, but by that Original Wiſdom wherewith he was created, (by the *Socinians* leave,) and a great part whereof he loſt by the Fall; for which reaſon theſe Names are the moſt *noble Monuments of Antiquity* we have left in the World. Thus to inſtance in a few; the *Camel*, a Creature which keeps its Name almoſt in all Languages, and which *Varro* himſelf grants to be taken from the *Syriack Language.* 'Tis derived from the *Hebrew* word *Gamal*, which ſignifies to *retribute*, or *repay*, either *good* or *evil*, for both of which the *Camel* is ſtill noted as the moſt tenacious of any animal. The Hebrew name of the Horſe is derived from a root, which ſignifies to rule, to *guide*, to *moderate*, and 'tis notorious this Creature is the moſt *docile*, and moſt eaſily ruled, conſidering its vaſt ſtrength, of any other.

The *Aſs* is derived from a word which ſignifies *Red*, of which colour they generally are in the Eaſt, a *White Aſs* being it ſeems a Rarity; the Judges and Great perſons uſually for ſtate riding upon 'em, as we ſee in the Song of *Deborah*: another name of the Aſs is taken from his *ſtrength*, which is undeniably more than any other Creatures of the ſame bulk. The Bull or Oxe derives its Name from a word that ſignifies *firmneſs*, or *ſtability*; 'tis in the Hebrew *Sor*, for which the *Chaldees* read *Thor*, the *Arabians Thaur*, whence undoubtedly the Greek and Latin, ταῦρος, and *Taurus.* The *Goat* from a word that denotes *roughneſs*, ——— The *Swine* from another, alluding to the *ſmallneſs of his Eyes*; the Dog *Celeb*, from the Heb. *Club*, and the *Arabian Calub*, which ſignifie a pair of Tongs or Pincers, from the *firmneſs* of his *Teeth* and *holdfaſt*, ſo remarkable that a true Maſtiffe will let his Legs be cut off, as has been try'd, before hee'l quit his hold — To inſtance in no more, tho' 'twere eaſie from the forementioned Author to run through all ſorts of Creatures, and after the ſame way prove their Originals. And we make no doubt but the ſame thing might be done by moſt *words* as well as the Names of theſe Creatures; we mean, that all or moſt other Languages, at leaſt in our part of the World, are deriv'd from thence, as *Avenarius* has endeavour'd to make good throughout his whole *Lexicon*, and that in many, and we think moſt words, with at leaſt as little or leſs violence than our common Etymologiſts uſe in works of that Nature, when they'd fetch the original of their words nearer hand. And tho' it may be true, that Learned Men may ſometimes ſtretch things farther than they'll go, by indulging too much to their Fancies, eſpecially in theſe Etymologies; yet we think the forecited Great Man (we mean *Bochart*) has prov'd the *Punic* and *Phœnician Language* to be all one, and both a Dialect of the Hebrew, and moſt of the Names of Countries, Iſlands, Promontories, and remarkable places in *Europe*, as well as further, from them to have taken their Originals; as among the reſt our own Iſland, the Etymology of which from *Baratanak*, anſwerable to the *Caſſiterides* of the *Greeks*, no Learned Man is now ignorant of. However, thus much we are certain of, that all or moſt other Languages are viſibly de-

7.3 cm (2.87 in)

**Figure 3.** *The Athenian Mercury* (1691). Private collection, M. J. M. Ezell.

of the new periodical that Dunton in the second issue of the fledging paper, he had already envisioned the spin-off product which would include both a preface and an index, both of which McEwen describes as "innovations" for English periodicals.[71] Dunton also promised the reader of his memoirs that they would also be able to purchase *Athenian Mercury* merch, "a choice Collection of the most valuable Questions and Answers, in Three Volumes."[72] Dunton also produced multiple supplements which were bound into the volumes offering the purchaser extra value: The first supplement contained information about "transactions and experiments of the Forreign Virtuoso's [*sic*]," and an account of "most of the considerable Books *Printed in all Languages*; and of the Quality of the Author, if known," in addition to translations of excerpts from learned journals such as the Paris *Journal des Scavans* and "in the New Book Entituled, *Entretiens Seriuses & Galantes, &c*."[73] Towards the end of his career, Dunton attempted to revive the brand, publishing four volumes of yet more questions and answers under the title of *The Athenian Oracle* (1703–1710).

The Athenian model of soliciting content in terms of questions, puzzles, and poetry was so successful, it soon attracted imitators, adapters, and satirists. The Grub Street writer Tom Brown (1662–1704) did a satirical counterpart, initially called the *London Mercury*, which quickly became *Lacedemonian Mercury* in February 1692/93. Brown, who earned his precarious living exploiting whatever genre was popular at the moment, deliberately tied his publication to Dunton's periodical by titling after Athens' ancient rival and enemy, the Lacedemonians (Spartans). Initially assisted in this effort by his friends Charles Gildon and William Pate, Brown released the first issue on Monday February 1, and brazenly announced that would it answer all questions sent to its preferred coffee house, Welsh's, near Temple Bar. As commentators have noticed, being published on Mondays and Friday, it thus could beat the *Athenian Mercury*'s responses which were printed on Tuesdays and Saturdays.[74] The University educated Brown ruthlessly skewered what he considered to be the overly pedantic and serious tone of Dunton's periodical, especially as it busied "the Press with impertinent Questions of Apprentices and Chamber-maids," and, rather than tackling serious intellectual issues of history and philosophy, "they have everlastingly stuff'd their Papers with Receipts for Fleas &c and such like."[75] Continuing this unflattering attention given to Dunton's periodical, Elkanah Settle, the dramatist and City Poet in charge of writing the annual pageants celebrating London's prestige and prosperity, published in 1693 *The New Athenian Comedy*. In it, Settle mocks the pseudointellectualism of "coffee-house culture" and the social status of its members;

[71] Gilbert D. McEwen, *The Oracle of the Coffee House*, p. 49.
[72] Dunton, *Life and Errors*, I: 194.
[73] *The Supplement to the First Volume of the Athenian Gazette* (1691), title page.
[74] McEwen, *The Oracle of the Coffee House*, pp. 35–36.
[75] Quoted in McEwen, *The Oracle of the Coffee House*, p. 37.

Settle's characters underscore Brown's mockery of the Athenians' membership, with names such as Obabia Grub, the leader, and Dorothy Tickleteat, a milkmaid.

## 2.4 Peter Motteaux and the Gentleman's Journal

A year after Dunton launched his periodical, the professional writer Peter Anthony Motteaux (1663–1718) started the *Gentleman's Journal*, which enjoyed thirty-three issues between 1692–1694. Born Pierre-Antoine Le Motteux in 1663 in Rouen, the young Huguenot had fled France in 1685 after the revocation of the Edict of Nantes and joined a large French refugee population in London. Although he is probably best known today as the translator of both Rabelais and Cervantes and whose death was the subject of a notorious murder trial, Motteux's pursued a varied career as a shopkeeper, auctioneer, dramatist, and librettist during the last decade of the seventeenth century.[76] Motteux's was a monthly periodical, which instead of being the front and back of a single-sheet, was a quarto pamphlet averaging around thirty pages (Figure 4). This expanded format offered the reader a variety of short reading entertainments, including verse by popular contemporary London poets such as the soon to be poet Laureate Nathum Tate, Aphra Behn, Matthew Prior, John Phillips, the ever-busy Charles Gildon, and the dramatist William Congreve. In addition, it also featured accounts of new plays, information about national events and personalities, such as the Duke of Bavaria being made the Governor of Spanish Netherlands, as well as new songs, complete with musical scores.

Motteux dedicated the first issue to the Earl of Devonshire, announcing the desire the little journal should "attend your Lordship when you enter into your Closet, to disengage your Thoughts from the daily pressure of Business."[77] While its title page describes the contents of consisting of "News, History, Philosophy, Poetry, Musick, Translations, &c," poetry, songs, and translation dominate the pages, not news. Told in the form of a familiar letter from a Londoner to his friend in the countryside, the *Gentleman's Journal* breaks with this narrative when in the next issue, it opens with an advertisement preceding the table of contents stating that the author has had so many letters commenting on the first issue that he cannot answer them all, but he promises to insert his readers' observations and contributions as long as they do not libel any one or speak against "Religion, or good Manners."[78] The narrator opens this

---

[76] See Cunningham, *Peter Anthony Motteux, 1663–1718.*

[77] "Epistle Dedicatory," *The Gentleman's Journal: Or, the Monthly Miscellany*, January 1692, Issue 1.

[78] *Gentleman's Journal*, February 1692.

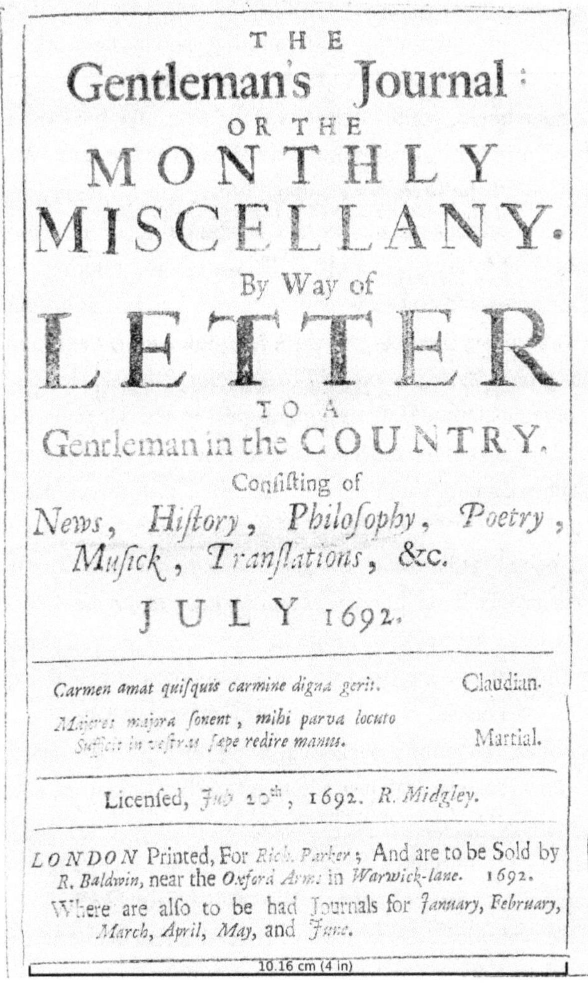

THE

Gentleman's Journal:

OR THE

MONTHLY

MISCELLANY.

By Way of

LETTER

TO A

Gentleman in the COUNTRY.

Conſiſting of

*News, Hiſtory, Philoſophy, Poetry, Muſick, Tranſlations,* &c.

JULY 1692.

*Carmen amat quiſquis carmine digna gerit.* Claudian.

*Majores majora ſonent, mihi parva locuto*
*Sufficit in veſtras ſæpe redire manus.* Martial.

Licenſed, *July* 20th, 1692. *R. Midgley.*

*LONDON* Printed, For *Rich. Parker*; And are to be Sold by *R. Baldwin*, near the *Oxford Arms* in *Warwick-lane*. 1692.
Where are alſo to be had Journals for *January, February, March, April, May*, and *June*.



**Figure 4.** The *Gentleman's Journal* (1692).
Private collection, M. J. M. Ezell.

"letter" to his friend observing that the "Generality of Readers lik'd the Design of the Book" and that several "ingenious Pieces . . . have been given me," such as the poem which follows that is attributed to the fashionable Matthew Prior (1664–1721) ("Howe'r; 'tis well, that whilst Mankind,/ Thro' Fates Fantastick Mazes errs"), and an imitation of one of Horace's Odes, "given me by a Friend" (5–6, 9). The appeal to the reader to become a contributor, to send by post their or their ingenious friends' poems, enigmas, and fictions, as I have argued elsewhere, is a step further than Dunton's request for queries: by urging his readers to become active content makers for his periodical publication, Motteux is essentially commercializing the traditional practice of coterie or social authorship, with its circulating and curating social network's manuscript pieces.[79]

As critics have noted, while Dunton was indeed in the business of books, he was not himself primarily a professional writer, as was Motteux. Walter Graham in his early study of the literary periodical noted that Motteux was, "a man of letters [and] for the first time the literary periodical as in the hands of professional writers."[80] Motteux's literary skills were wide ranging – he not only translated Cervantes and Rabelais, but he also wrote prologues and epilogues for multiple dramatists including George Farquhar, John Vanbrugh, Mary Pix, and songs for Aphra Behn's comedy *The Younger Brother*. He also had several of his own tragedies, comedies, and operas performed. He achieved a measure of commercial success in the most popular Restoration literary enterprises, even if his biographer Robert Cunningham described him as having "versatility" rather than brilliance.[81] Pragmatically, Motteux knew what would sell; to meet this demand, he skillfully attracted a group of amateur contributors as well as calling on his professional literary acquaintances to create the contents. As I argued elsewhere, Motteux was able to secure and sustain the *Gentleman's Journal* for three years in part through his recognizing and exploiting the characteristics of coterie, social authorship practices within a commercial framework, not unlike today's participatory culture.[82]

Some of the elements that characterized earlier social or coterie literary exchanges included the use of pen names, the popularity of response pieces, and the feeling of community or familiarity among the writers and readers. Motteux used a direct form of appeal: The "Advertisement" below the table of contents of the Volume 2, issue 5 May, 1693 desired that "the Ingenious are desir'd to send such Pieces in Verse or Prose that may properly be inserted in this Miscellany." These can be left at the shops of either of the booksellers mentioned on the title page, Richard Parker at the Unicorn under the Piazza at the Royal Exchange or Robert Baldwin's near the Oxford Arms in Warwick-lane. Parker was a successful young bookseller in the fashionable Royal Exchange, while Baldwin, along with his wife Anne (who continued his business after his death in 1698 and published the *Female Tatler* to be discussed in the next section), was among the best known of the London printers and bookbinders of this decade, publishing not only political pamphlets, satires, and periodicals but also plays and romances. In addition, those who wished to contribute

79 See Ezell, "*The Gentleman's Journal*."

80 Graham, *English Literary Periodicals*, p. 55.

81 Cunningham, *Peter Anthony Motteux, 1663–1718*, pp. 195, 201–05.

82 Ezell, "*The Gentleman's Journal*." On the term "participatory culture," see Jenkins et al, "Confronting the Challenges of Participatory Culture."

but did not live in near the two booksellers or in London, could address a letter to the "Author" of the *Gentleman's Journal* at the Black-Boy Coffee-house in Ave-Maria Lane, "not forgetting to discharge the Postage."

Among the contributions published in the May 1692 issue were a satire, "they came to me out of the Country . . . I am not told who is their Author," the correct solution to the enigma poem in the previous issue answered in verse by Mr. Jon. Olt, which was also correctly solved by "Aurelia," T. S., T. Powell, and "S. Strephon."[83] A new enigma poem was sent to Motteux by "Philander" in "Edenburgh": "An unborn Queen of Sweets and Beauties I,/ Still blushing, and still smiling, live and die./ In richest Robes of purest Light, I shine;/ And all my happy Nourishment's divine." The answer as revealed in the June issue is a rose and it inspired Mr. Patrick Johnson to address verses "To the Ladies on the Enigma for May": "A Darker Riddle, Ladies, ne'er you knew/ 'Tis hard to guess what's meant, a Rose, or You." This type of literary game offered readers the chance to participate in a literary network outside their immediate family and friends.

Relying on the ingenious readers for content, however, could be unpredictable. In March of 1692, Motteux informs his fictious acquaintance in the country that he is running out of materials to be included, laboring as he says under the "necessity there is of a constant Supply of Ingenious Prose and Poetry, to carry on the Undertaking."[84] "I hope, Sir," Motteux observes, that "the Ingenious of both Sexes will maturely consider of the Exigency of the Case. For tho' I have had several very fine things sent Me: yet I shall have occasion for more, and some things, as I declared it in my last Month's Advertisement, tho' never so ingenious, I cannot insert." The content of Motteux's *Journal* was, like the initial form of the *Philosophical Transactions*, largely dependent on what the editor could persuade his network of friends and correspondents to contribute, balanced out by his own works; the September 1692 and the July 1693 issues were entirely Motteux's own work.[85]

The *Gentleman's Journal*, more than the *Athenian Mercury*, focused on literary matters, in particular what was "new." In addition to publishing a wide range of contemporary poets, the *Gentleman's Journal* is unique in including not only the lyrics to new songs, but also the scores. During its two-year run, the *Journal* printed twenty songs by the celebrated musician Henry Purcell.[86] It also included a notable amount of short fiction, some thirty-six narratives that appeared under various titles ranging from "adventure," "story," "True History," "fable," and "novel." Critics from the beginning of their

[83] *Gentleman's Journal*, May 1692, p. 161. [84] *Gentleman's Journal*, March 1692.
[85] Foster, "The Earliest Precursor of Our Present-Day Monthly Miscellanies," p. 28.
[86] Radice, "Henry Purcell's Contributions to the *Gentleman's Journal*," p. 25.

commentary on this periodical have observed that the fictions are about contemporary people, places, and events, with Dorothy Foster arguing in 1917 that they "portray contemporary types, contemporary manners," and Coperías-Aguilar in 2022 pointing to the degree to which the plots and character types have been drawn from contemporary social comedies that stressed realistic settings and characters.[87] As Coperías-Aguilar observes, the framing narrative that shapes the *Journal* and its contents, a fictive letter from a friend in London to a person in the city to keep them *au currant* with fashionable topics, music, and literature, "enhanced the fictionality of the 'novels' and also reinforced their condition of true stories."[88]

There is no evidence at present that the periodicals discussed in this section paid their contributors – as we have seen even warning them that they would not cover the cost of the Penny Post – although it would be reasonable to expect that other professional writers and musicians such as Wycherley and Handel might be. Instead, to generate content, they relied on creating a sense of community in their general reading audience, encouraging them to become content creators, and voluntarily to share their questions, literary works, and discoveries. It is clear, of course, that from the publishers' and editors' perspectives, the journals from their first conceptualization were intended to make a profit, and Dunton was particularly ingenious in devising ways in which his readers' curiosity could be monetized. When the readers' interest slacked and their contributions declined, the periodical ceased publication. As we shall explore in the next section, the periodicals that followed them preserved many of the features of this participatory, active audience which characterize the periodicals of the end of the seventeenth century, but as we shall see, with increasing commercial considerations for the writers.

## 3 Sociable Periodicals, 1700s–1720s, Continuity and Change: Aaron Hill's the *British Apollo*, the *Female Tatler*, and Daniel Defoe's the *Review*

> . . . [news] media faces a scenario marked by global instability, economic crisis, misinformation, falling trust and renewed consumption habits with a specific challenge to reach young audiences. This scenario implies experimenting with channels, technologies and formats, to approach such an audience in an innovative, attractive, friendly, simple and fun way.
>
> –Jorge Vázquez-Herrero et al. – "Let's dance the news! How the news media are adapting to the logic of TikTok" (2020)[89]

[87] Foster, "The Earliest Precursor of Our Present-Day Monthly Miscellanies," p. 45.
[88] Coperías-Aguilar, "Between Fictionality and Reality," p. 10.
[89] Vázquez et al. "Let's Dance the News!"

Two periodicals and a challenger to one highlight strategies used by what I am calling sociable periodicals to cultivate and sustain a subscribing participating readership over a long period of time. They did so in part by combining attractive features of their predecessors the *Athenian Mercury* and the *Gentleman's Journal* with new types of content presentation and new marketing strategies to encourage readers to become paying followers rather than merely enjoying the copies offered for entertainment at public houses and helping to create its content. The *British Apollo*, which appeared twice weekly on Wednesdays and Fridays 1708–1709, then additionally on Mondays until 1711, was overseen by the poet Aaron Hill. It engaged in a lively literary spat with the upstart *Female Tatler* (July 1709–1710) for several months, August 1709 through early October, over some of its tactics to lure paying subscribers, including the use of music, and the quarrel between the two offers some revealing glimpses of the competition for readers as well as how the readers of this early form social media were viewed by the public at large.

Daniel Defoe's periodical, the *Review*, originally titled *A Review of the Affairs of FRANCE* (October 1704–February 1705), was also initially published twice weekly, increasing to three times per week 1704–1713. Significantly, Defoe made use of the new, expanding postal system, and his paper appeared on Tuesdays, Thursday, and Saturdays, the same days that the Post Office in Lombard Street in London sent the post to all the English counties. As J. A. Downie points out, this means Defoe from the beginning was envisioning a national audience rather than a London one, that the periodical "appears to have been designed for distribution throughout England from the outset."[90] As we shall see, while Defoe initially made use of several of the expected conventions of the sociable journal at the beginning of his periodical which was devoted to news of international affairs and domestic politics, over time the content as well as the relationship between the author and his readers would change.

## 3.1 Aaron Hill and the British Apollo, Mrs. Crackenthorpe and the Female Tatler, and the Battle over Readers

A decade after Dunton's question and answer periodical stopped publishing, there was apparently sufficient demand again that another aspiring literary man, Aaron Hill, offered the public *The British Apollo*, which ran from February 1709 to 1711 [Figure 5]. This placed the *British Apollo* in direct competition with Steele's the *Tatler*, which used a much different format and rapport with its target audience, which will be discussed in the next section. In

[90] Downie, "Stating Facts Right about Defoe's Review," p. 16.

Numb. 77.

# The British Apollo,

OR,

*Curious Amuſements for the INGENIOUS.*

To which are added the moſt

Material Occurrences Foreign and Domeſtick.

*Perform'd by a Society of GENTLEMEN.*

From Wedneſday November 3d. to Friday November 5th. 1708.

Q. *Gentlemen, Your Opinion is deſir'd, whether or no Children, that are born of Unbelieving Parents, and dye in their Infancy, have any Sin to anſwer for, but Original Sin.*

*A.* The Purport of your Queſtion returns to this; namely, whether the Children of Unbelieving Parents, who dye in their Infancy, ſhall ſuffer for their Parents Neglect, or Unbelief. In anſwer to which, we need no more than recite thoſe *words of Truth and Soberneſs ; the Soul, that ſinneth, That ſhall dye.*

Q. *Whether Confirmation be ſufficient to one, that never was Baptiz'd ?*

*A.* The Ordinance you ſpeak of, is therefore ſtil'd *Confirmation*, becauſe it *Confirms* the Previous Sacrament of Baptiſm. But now we deſire to know, whether *That* can be *Confirm'd*, which has *no Being*.

Q. *Does the Devil know our Thoughts ?*

*A.* To Know our Thoughts is repreſented in the Scriptures as the Incommunicable Prerogative of that Omniſcient God, who is a *Searcher of the Heart*. The Devil therefore can no otherwiſe Dive into our Thoughts, than as by the Sagacity of his Nature he can lay Concurring Circumſtances together, and Draw Appoſite Concluſions from them.

Q. *Gentlemen, If the Divinity of our Saviour had no ſhare in his Sufferings, why would not any other Man have made as ſufficient an Atonement, for the Sins of Mankind, as himſelf.*

*A.* The Merits of the Manhood ( which Alone was Capable of Suffering ) receiv'd an Ineſtimable Value by the Honor of ſo Intimate an Union with the God-head.

Q. *About five Years ago I was unfortunately married to a Man ( who unknown to me ) had a Wife then living ; after I had lived with him near a Year, 'twas diſcovered, and I immediately went from him, and he ſoon after left his Wife again, and has not been heard of ſince : I deſire to know whether I may lawfully marry again, I having had no Child by him A ſpeedy Anſwer will oblige Yours*, &c.

*A.* You are no More His Wife, than if you were Never Married to him ; and therefore as Free to Marry Another, as when you were a Maid.

7.2 cm (2.83 in)

Q. *Gentlemen, Being encouraged by your ſeveral Pertinent and Ingenious Anſwers, perſuant to the Queſtions directed to You ; I have made bold to ask your Opinion in a matter ſomewhat dubiouſly related ( viz. ) What Nation, after* Noah's *general Deluge, firſt us'd a Monarchial Government ? Your Anſwer will not only Highly Satisfie, but ſuperlatively oblige Your Admirer*, &c.

*A.* Aſſyria.

The Queſtion ſent us concerning *David* and *Jonathan*, is ſo obvious in it's Natural Conſtruction, that we can ſcarcely forbear ſuſpecting, that the Author wou'd turn it to a Wanting Senſe. If he Does, that of *Terence* may be a ſufficient Anſwer, *Mala Mens, Malus Animus :* An Ill Mind, an Ill Meaning.

Q. *Gentlemen, I deſire you'll inform me, in what manner ( if one Wiſpers againſt the Wall on one ſide in the Cupulo of* St. Pauls ) *the Voice is retorted ſo very much louder to the other.*

*A.* Sounds are Communicated in Arcuate Lines, and therefore Arcuate Fabricks ( ſuch as the Wall you ſpeak of) are more Agreeable to their Extenſive Propagation.

Q. *Gentlemen, I never troubl'd you yet with any Queſtion, ſo I hope you'll ſpeedily ſolve this : I ever have been told, that being born with a* Cawl *was a Token of good luck, hitherto I have ſeen none, I'm* 22 *and ſee no Husband come, no not one Woer, I'm afraid I'll lead Apes in Hell.* Now, *pray tell me, your Opinion thereon, and from whence proceeds that Notion of the fortune of being born with a* Cawl, *and why they attribute ſo many good qualities to it. Silvia.*

*A.* We muſt own, Good Mrs. *Silvia*, 'tis a thouſand Pities you ſhould ſuffer under this Diſappointment, and ſpend ſo many *Luſtrums* without having ſo much as one Squeak for a Husband : But as your Affliction took its riſe from the Vanity of your Early Hopes in the *Succeſsleſs Cawl*, whereby you have Contracted Dreadful Apprehenſions of a Stygian Office, ſo we deſire you would aſſure your ſelf, that this Notion is altogether Groundleſs, and firſt trumpt up by fancyful and Superſtitious Old Women ; the *Cawl* being nothing elſe but a Portion of the Membrane *Amnios*, which ſometimes cleaves to the Head, and is there diſcover'd at the Time of Birth.

Hhhh Q. Gentle-

**Figure 5.** *The British Apollo* (1708). Private collection. M. J. M. Ezell.

its first issue, the *British Apollo. Or, Curious Amusements for the Ingenious. To which are added the most Material Occurrences Foreign and Domestick. Perform'd by a Society of Gentlemen* announced confidently to its potential subscribers that it would appear on Wednesday and Fridays, and that the Society of Gentlemen would

> answer all Questions in Divinity, Philosophy, the Mathematicks, and other Arts and Sciences, which appear fit and worthy to be answer'd; Also insert Poems on various Subjects and Occasions, both Serious and Comical, Compos'd New Purposely for the Paper.[91]

On the title page of the subsequent volumes of the collected issues of the *British Apollo*, it is notable that the description of the membership of this "Society of Gentleman," in fact apparently led by Hill and later assisted by John Gay (the future author of the *Beggar's Opera*), is expanded: The answers are "approved of by many of the Most Learned and Ingenious of both Universities, and of the Royal Society." No doubt the prestige of association with the learned society and university dons might appeal to potential purchasers of this handsome production, which by 1741 comprised three collected volumes and a fourth edition, featuring a dozen pages of prefatory verses contributed by admirers of both sexes. Among Hill's other known associates answering questions were the physician to Queen Anne, Sir John Arbuthnot; Marshall Smith, a poet who would go on in 1715 to propose another periodical, *The Oracle, being calculated for the answering questions in all arts and sciences, either serious, comical, or humerous [sic], both in prose and poetry*; the physician and theological writer Dr. William Coward, and Dr. James Mauclerc, a member of the College of Physicians, who would in 1745 publish *The Christian Magazine* discussing a wide range of theological matters. Were they paid for their answers? At this point we don't know.

As with the *Athenian Mercury*, the questions posed in each issue of the *British Apollo* were wide ranging in topic and seemingly random in sequence. Inquirers in the first issue wanted to know why God took six days to create the earth rather than do it instantaneously; in later issues, readers demanded to know when and why the custom of "throwing at Cocks on Shrove-Tuesday" arose. Readers were interested in the size of the moon compared to the size of the earth and why when one drinks turpentine it causes urine to smell like violets. There were also some more romantically inclined queries: "Tell, me, O! Tell me, What is Happiness?" drew the poetic response, "If Madam, yet some Husbands arm you bless, /Ask Him, for He, if any, sure can guess."

[91] *British Apollo,* no. 1, February 13, 1709.

Ten months later, by the December 3–8, 1709 issue, the journal was well established and offered its readers a characteristic range of content comprised of a balance of queries, poetry, news, and advertising. By this time, it had also published a separate quarterly collection, also for sale by the printer of the *British Apollo*, to which it could refer readers asking the more common questions, such as "of what sort of Fruits, was the Forbidden Tree?"[92] Also in this issue is a lengthy melancholy tale from a young man. This is less a question than a short fiction: The sad and perplexed gentleman has fallen in love with a young lady of a different religion, but his father opposes the match, stating it would break his heart as well as cause them to forfeit their family estate; the father proposes another more suitable match; the true object of his affection urges him to obey his father's wishes, although she declares this will cause *her* to die of a broken heart. The letter concludes "we have both agreed to follow your Directions." The answer from the Gentlemen is not to propose to the suitable Other Woman, but to wait and hope time sorts things out, for, although all parties will be made miserable by this, "your Conscience and Honour will be satisfy'd, not without a Possibility in time of Satisfaction al all Parties."

This romantic conundrum is followed by an unromantic query about the cause of snoring. That pragmatic domestic question is given a brief and straightforward answer. The next section of the issue is composed of a series of questions posed and answered in verse. The first verse petition of the journal, strikingly, is in the voice of a young African:

> From Africk's scorching Sands my place of Birth,
> In my Younger Years transpos'd to Britian's Isle,
> By all esteem'd the happiest Isle on Earth,
> For Beauty, Pleasure, and a fruitful soil.
> Thus hither brought, I by my Master's care
> In way of Traffick, did Instructions learn.
> Thus he did readily my Mind prepare,
> Mankind by Conversation to discern.

The problem is that in these conversations, the Christian religion has remained merely a name to the writer. "My Fellow Creatures tell me" that after death they will be returned to Africa, but in contrast, Christians speak of going after death to "Realms of Bliss and Regions of Delight." The question posed by the poet is if he, or she, might go to heaven, too, and, if so, how? The response, also in verse, is a resounding yes: to achieve a Christian Heaven, the African poet must first read the Scriptures, those "Oracles Divine," and only then converse further with Christians; eventually thus will the petitioner come to "feel the Blessings of

[92] *British Apollo*, n. 86, 3–8, December 1709.

Unsullied Day/ And Hug th' Enjoyment of a Peaceful Mind." Was this poem really written by a young person of color?[93] We have no way of knowing at this point, but regardless, it was a topic which the society of "gentlemen" of the *British Apollo* felt was worthy of addressing and would be of interest to their readers.

The *British Apollo* exerted itself to create a sense of select community and privilege among its subscribers, including making its quarterly collections and supplements available first to its subscribers only. In another attempt to market the periodical, to increase paying subscribers, while sustaining a sense of social networking community, the publishers hit upon a scheme which initially seemed very attractive, but which would backfire spectacularly. As Rosamund McGuinness notes "the *British Apollo* was eager to appease its readers and to be seen to be so … us[ing] its amenability as an additional selling point."[94] Responding to requests from several ladies and gentleman, it began in July 1709 to advertise it would publish not only new songs but new music to go with them, which as we have seen, the *Gentleman's Journal* had done previously. The *British Apollo* initially published only the vocal line of the song, without all the instrumental ones, because of space; one could, however, acquire all the musical parts, at the shop of "Mr. Walsh in Katherine-Street against Somerset House" (October, 1709). In August of 1709, the periodical announced that its Subscribers of more than a quarter of a year would be eligible to get tickets for "a Grand Consort" of their music, which was quickly amended to those who had subscribed already for a half a year. The Concerts never took place, possibly for financial reasons.

The poet Nicholas Rowe found the prospect of the periodical including music delightful. He enthused that

> Apollo now in full Meridian Shines,
> By joyning Music to his Tuneful Lines.
> Before y'improv'd our Minds with Notions new,
> But now you Charm our Souls and Senses too. (10–12 August 1709)

As we have seen, including the lyrics and basic melodies to new songs, especially those written for the London theatres, had proved a popular final section of the *Gentleman's Journal*. Not all readers, however, were so taken with the idea of including music and, in particular, of offering possible musical entertainments for

93 An estimated 20,000 Africans were living in England in the first decades of the eighteenth century. Many Black residents had been brough as children to work as servants, such as an unnamed African in the household of a West Indies merchant, https://secretlibraryleeds.net/2021/10/07/before-windrush-black-people-in-leeds-bradford-1708-1948-part-i/. Advertisements in the *British Apollo* also make mention of "blackamore" servants.

94 McGuiness, "Musical Provocation in Eighteenth-Century London: The 'British Apollo,'" p. 333.

the pleasure of the *British Apollo*'s London subscribers. A lively, controversial new periodical paper had come to life as a counterpart to Steele's *Tatler*, the *Female Tatler*, written by one "Mrs. Crackenthorpe, a Lady that knows every thing" [Figure 6]. The identity of those involved with this periodical has long vexed literary historians, as it appeared under the same title simultaneously in two versions, one published by Benjamin Bragge in Paternoster Row, and the other published by Anne Baldwin at the Oxford Arms in Warwick Lane. These rival *Female Tatlers* were identical in format and numbering but different in content. The authorship of the periodicals has been variously ascribed to a minor dramatist Thomas Baker, according to the *British Apollo*, and by later generations of literary historian as possibly being the work of the philosopher and satirist Bernard Mandeville (author of the satire *The Fable of the Bees*), and recently the dramatist and political journalist Delarivier Manley.[95]

In Issue 11, August 22–24, 1709, published by Bragge, there was an account of a visit by "Lady Sly" who mocked the idea of including music in a question-and-answer paper. "After a world of dull, indigested incoherent Stuff" inflicted on their readers, she observes, now they intend to publish musical scores, but whom among their readers, Lady Sly wonders, will know what they are? "Does one in five hundred understand Notes? The Dissenters will swear 'tis Popery in Hebrew Characters, and their Subscribers at Wapping think it down-right Witchcraft," she cackles, but "the best jest is, they are to have a Consort, an't please you, and ev'ry Subscriber is to have a Right to a Ticket." Just imagine the scene at the concert, she urges her listener/reader, "there must be a noble Appearance, his Grace and my Lady Dutchess, Jack Tar, and Mrs. Top-gallant-sail, with every Coffee-Man, and his Wife, that takes in their Papers."

As Robert White observes, "the *Female Tatler* had begun the fight, but the *Apollo* was to win it."[96] [Figure 6a] After a lively exchange of insults over the relative merits of the two publications and their readerships, the *Female Tatler* published by Baldwin on August 31–September 2, 1709 claimed that when Mrs. Crackenthorpe sent a servant to find issues of the *British Apollo* to see what had been written about her in it, "no Booksellers had 'em, the chief

[95] See White, *A Study of the Female Tatler* for a discussion of the rival periodicals, especially Section 2. It considers the Bragge publications to be the "real" *Female Tatler*, with the ones published by Anne Baldwin "spurious." Starting with issue # 19, August 19, 1709, Bragge and Baldwin published simultaneous identically numbered issues with differing content. Bragge dropped out in October with issue number 44, but Baldwin continued through November with issue 51 where "Mrs. Crackthorpe" announces she is turning the periodical over to a "Society of Ladies" to write; this lasted until issue # 111, March 31, 1710. See Graham, "Thomas Aker, Mrs. Manley, and the *Female Tatler*," Smith, "Thomas Baker and the Female Tatler." For Manley, see Anderson, "The History and Authorship of Mrs. Crackenthorpe's *Female Tatler.*" This will be further discussed in the next section.

[96] White, *A Study of the Female Tatler*, p. 368.

Numb. 7.

# The Female Tatler.

*By Mrs.* Crackenthorpe, *a Lady that knows every thing.*

*Sum Canna Vocalis.*

From *Wednesday July* 20. to *Friday July* 22.

Esterday being my *Visiting-day*, I had the most agreeable select Sett of Company, that ever yet grac'd my *Drawing-room*. Our Discourse ran chiefly upon the different manner of People's Behaviour in Publick; their Birth, their Education, their Dispositions; what is *Nature*, and what *Affectation*, are easily discover'd by their way of Address; that as the most rustical Habit cannot hide the *fine Gentleman*, nor the gayest Embroidery give an Air to the *Clown*; so true Wit and Breeding, notwithstanding all modest Endeavours to conceal 'em, will, to People of Observation, discover themselves from the vain Pretences of Impertinence, and fluttering Assurance, A *Sophister* may pass upon the generality for a Man of Learning, a prating *Quack* for a great Physician, and a conceited *Punster* for a Youth of quick Repartee; but Persons, who have truly study'd Mankind, dart thro' such false Appearances; and to make a right Judgment of Things in so deceitful an Age, is a Happiness inexpressible, both for Admiration and Ridicule.-------Lady *Courtly* charms me with her obliging Carriage; her Humility will seat her any where, rather than disturb the Company; her Conversation is easy and affable, she neither ingrosses the whole Talk to her self, nor sits silent to make splenitick Observations: She's so far from reflecting upon any body, and so very good, that when absent Persons are taken to pieces, if they have but one tolerable Quality, she says it, if not, she not only holds her Tongue, but gives a pretty Interruption to the *Scandal*, with,------*Has your Ladyship any Snuff*,---- *the sweetest Box I ever saw*,-----and so courteous to the meanest Servant, that her Condescension exalts her above her Quality; her Demeanour shows, she's of an ancient Family, truly bred, Benign, Hospitable, Charitable, and would rather suffer a very great Prejudice to her self, than to do the least ill Office to another.------Lady *Stately* is her Reverse; she raises the whole Room, and then squats down above her Betters, without paying the least Respect to any body; she looks askew for half an Hour, without speaking a Word, then rails at the whole Town, and very often at the Government; finds Fault with People's Cloaths, 'till they are forc'd to leave the Room; and if any Lady offers at her Snuff box, she flings the rest into the Fire before her Face; her Wit is equal to her Manners, she tells you a Story of her self, when she was a Girl, and never condescends to laugh but at her own Jests; she's so very imperious, her Lord is hardly good enough to approach her, her Servants are her Slaves, and she'll send one of 'em ten Miles a foot to know how her *Dutch* Dog does. She was an Admiral's Widow bred at *Yarmouth*, worth thirty Thousand Pounds, and meeting with a decay'd Noble man, her Mony made her a Woman of Quality; by her, you may judge a little of Upstart Grandeur.

Our Discourse ran next upon the City, and Mrs. *Ramble* told us, their Disposition was *to admire every Court Humour, and ridiculously to imitate it*; that she knew a Merchant's Wife affected Lady *Courtly*, and aim'd at general Esteem by a Mobbish Condescension; she'd visit *Barbers* and *Taylors* Wives, walk Arm in Arm with a *Mantua-Woman*, and put on all her Jewels to go to *Leaden-hall Market*, where she'd bawl out,-----*You, Puppy, what must you have for that Shoulder of Veal*,----*Three and Six Pence*, Madam.---*Why, you impudent Toad, I have bought a better for half a Crown, there's three Shillings for you, send it home this Moment; and do you hear, Scoundrel, if I find it blown up with a Quill, as you us'd to do, I'll break your Head, Sirrah, next time I come to Market.* They adore her for calling 'em Names, it puts her upon the Level with them.-----*Heaven's bless her Honour, she's a dear Lady, and not a bit of Pride in her.* We have our City-Lady *Statelies* too, termigant Dames, that eat Meat in a Morning, bully their Husbands, beat their Prentices, fling a Punch-Bowl at the Maid's Head, and then make her pay for't. And if their Husbands Riches advance 'em to City Honours, the haughtiest Court Lady has not half their Pride.

When *Chairs* ply'd first in the City, I was pleas'd to hear an Alderman's Lady bid her Man *Jehosophat* call her a *Sedan*; she went into *East-cheap* to make a Visit, but not being us'd to that sort of riding, was abominably sick by the way; but the greatest Misfortune was, when they set her down, she rose before the top of the *Chair* could be lifted up, and put her Neck out of Joint.

We drop'd that Stuff, and went upon the different Taste People of Rank have of Diversions. Sir *Charles Easy* reads the Pamphlets and the News, converses with Men of Sense, has Wit among the Ladies, sees a Play, drinks a moderate Bottle, and is a reasonable Creature in every thing. Sir *Noisy Parrot* plays at Quoits, and Nine-holes, flings at Cocks, Wrestles, and Rows upon the Thames, he's a Coxcomb in every thing; nay, I hear'd, that four *worthy Senators* lately threw their Hats into a River, laid a Crown each, whose Hat should swim first to the Mill, and ran hallowing after 'em; and he that won the Prize was in a greater Rapture, than if he had carry'd the most dangerous Point in Parliament. Lady *Easy* loves the best Company, and is valu'd by them, she reads a Novel, when alone, or a little Work, which other People think Business, is a mighty Pleasure to her; after Dinner, she plays a game at *Picquet*, and in the Evening, an *Opera*, or *Hide-Park*. Lady *Parrot* abominates Books; for Work, she'd as leave be hung up by the Heels as do a Stitch, the *Opera's* squawling Stuff, and the *Eunuch's* a nasty

Fellow;

**Figure 6.** *The Female Tatler*, no. 7 (1709). By permission of Harry Ransom Center, University of Texas, Austin.

Fellow; and for *Cards*, ſhe plays at nothing but *Putt*; the Joy of her Spirit is a merry Junqueting-bout; ſhe haunts all the *Wakes* in the Country; is at *Stur-bridge* and *Bury* Fair; ſhe'll ride threeſcore Miles to ſee a *Puppet-Show*, loves a Country Fiddle, if the Fellows play loud, and will dance a *Horn-pipe* of an Hour long.

The vulgar ſort are ſuppos'd to have vulgar Ideas; but for Perſons of Diſtinction, who have ſuch repeated Opportunities of Improvement, their Natures muſt be ſtrangely perverſe, when neither Precept, Example, nor Ridicule can model them into a genteel Habit.

Since I undertook this Paper, I have diſcover'd the Impertinence of the World to be infinitely greater than I could have imagin'd it: I receiv'd yeſterday above thirty Letters, in all which I could not make one tolerable Obſervation. They conſiſt of *ſilly Amours, petty Reflections, frivolous Tales*, and *ſcandalous Aſperſions*: Young People and Fools, think the TATLERS give 'em a mighty Opportunity to expoſe their Superiours; and when a Mother ſhall juſtly correct her Daughter, a Lady her Servants, or a Tradeſman his Prentices, they make no Reply, but Letters are immediately diſpatch'd to ridicule them in Print, Should ſuch People be encourag'd, a Paper of this kind would be not only Uſeleſs, but Pernicious, ſince moſt Families harbour a Detractor, and Maſters muſt be afraid to direct thoſe they feed, leſt they ſhould draw their Characters. But if Gentlemen or Ladies pleaſe to write any thing that may be ſerviceable to the Publick, it will be kindly receiv'd. The following Letter I think deſerves particular Notice:

rent Churches in a Service, which gives Diſturbance to thoſe united in Devotions, where inſtead of Attention, they ſtare about, make ſome ridiculous Obſervations, and are gone. Theſe Gentlemen little conſider one in every Church knows 'em, and tho' they want good Principles, they ought to be ſo kind to their Reputations, are not to tell it the whole Town.

*** *Mrs*, Crackenthorpe *gives her Service to the Authors of the* Britiſh Apollo, Review, Obſervator, Flying-Poſt, Engliſh-Poſt, *and* Supplement, *and does hereby diſcharge 'em from troubling the Town any longer, the Coffee-Houſes making heavy Complaints againſt 'em; neither does ſhe think it Reputeable, that her Paper ſhould be ſeen upon the Table in ſuch intolerable Company*,

††† *Mrs*. Crackenthorpe *has receiv'd the agreeable Letter from* Burgeridicius, *which ſhe'll take care to inſert in her next; and hopes the Author will be as good as his Word. But that ſhe may not be behind hand in Civility; takes this Opportunity of giving him an Invitation to her* Drawing-Room, *where he ſhall have an Elbow Chair and ſelect Company for his Entertainment*,

ADVERTISEMENTS,

* *The Accomptant's Aſſiſtant* in Vulgar and Decimal Arithmetick, Wherein the Principles and Practical Rules of both are ſo plainly (tho conciſely) deliver'd, as to qualify every Capacity, not only for her Majeſties Revenues of *Exciſe, Cuſtoms*, &c. but alſo for the Recreation of Gentlemen, Practice of Merchants and Bankers, and uſe of Tradeſmen, Schools, *&c*. By *Tho. Lydal* Accomptant to the Honourable Commiſſioners of Her

**Figure 6a.** *The Female Tatler*, no. 7 v (1709). By permission of Harry Ransom Center, University of Texas, Austin.

Coffee-houses have thrown 'em out these six Months, the Mercury Women laugh'd," while the *British Apollo* riposted that back issues of the *Female Tatler* could be purchased at 2 pennies "per Pound, to stock the Chandlers, Tobacco shops" as wrapping paper.[97] The *Female Tatler* published by Baldwin on August 31–September 2, rebuts the *Apollo*'s claim that everyone is used to audiences of mixed social status at the theatre and no one is offended, countering that "the *Theatre* has *Pit*, *Box* and *Galleries* for Distinction, and when the meaner sort have the assurance to crowd into best place, how they are jostl'd and ridicul'd." Mrs. Crackenthorpe notes that "at *Consorts* of Note the Prices are extravagant, purposedly to keep out inferior people":

> But as their Tickets are to be delivered gratis to each Subscriber, ev'ry Purse-proud Ale-Wife thinks her self as good as Quality, and as she does 'em as much Service, expects as forward a Seat; and what Woman o' Fashion will lessen her Character, or care to have her Cloathes sullied by sitting *Jig* by *Jole* with *Apollo*'s Taplashes [pub owner]: In short, they are a pack of very silly Fellows, do they so wonderfully praise themselves. (#25, August 31–September 2, Baldwin)

[97] Quoted in White, p. 367.

Attacking the readership of the periodical as being lower class social climbers presuming to appreciate elite culture clearly was a way to tarnish both its contents and the publishers. It is notable that a former collaborator of Hill's on the periodical, John Gay, after he ceased contributing also made snide comments about the social origins of the *British Apollo*'s readers, observing that "it still recommends itself by deciding wagers and cards, and giving good advice to shopkeepers and their apprentices."[98] As we will see Daniel Defoe was at some pains to establish that the readership of his periodical, the *Review* and its Supplements, was genteel, perhaps to ward off such damaging notions.

Musical controversies aside, the contents of the *British Apollo* have been a treasure trove for later generations of literary historians interested in how the periodical trade worked because it was so explicit in explaining to its readers how the journal operated. The early issues clearly lay out how much it would cost, who could be paid for subscriptions, where to send letters and advertisements, and where the subscriber could purchase the growing number of additional items that were associated with it. As William Belcher noted in his 1957 article, the *British Apollo* was perhaps the first periodical that operated on a subscription scheme and he attributes the careful explanations carried in each issue about how to obtain the paper and how to submit advertising were intended to guide "those who [were] unfamiliar with the details of this method of publication."[99] Instead of relying largely on the public coffee houses or inns to supply the periodical to their customers, the *British Apollo* would, for two shillings a quarter deliver the periodical to your house on Wednesdays and Fridays, as long as you resided within the area specified by the London Bills of Mortality (I,1, Friday, February 13, 1709). Interestingly, given the subsequent sneers at the social status of its readers after it was well established, from the first issue the *British Apollo* announced as an inducement to potential subscribers that "this Design was incourag'd by several Persons of Quality and others of the Brightest Parts, before it was Publish'd, and a great many Subscrib'd for it as soon as the Proposals were out."

To subscribe, according to the directions that appeared in the first issues, one should direct a letter for the *British Apollo* at its printer's shop, John Mayo, in Fleet Street. Mayo apparently kept the list of subscribers, and his shop also was one of the places where you could direct your letters containing queries for the club to answer. The bookseller William Keble in Westminster-Hall and Thomas Bickerton, a bookseller at the Golden Flower-de-luce, in St. Paul's Churchyard, additionally sold the *British Apollo* as single sheets and later as sets, and

[98] John Gay, *The Present State of Wit* (1711), p. 23.

[99] Belcher, "The Sale and Distribution of the British Apollo," p. 75.

would also accept advertisements and queries, but not requests for subscriptions. Following Dunton's lead, these outlets also handled the range of merchandize associated with the *British Apollo*, from missed single issues, title pages for collected issues, bound volumes with indexes and prefatory materials, to additional supplements with even more questions than had failed to make it in the original individual issues. Bickerton, for example, could supply one with the individual issues and planned monthly supplements for the journal and, until the loose issues could be bound, "books of Guards [folders holding 150 papers] to keep 'em in" at only two shillings a piece.[100]

Another key source of income for this turn of the century periodical was advertisements. In the first few issues, it was stated firmly that advertisements from "quacks" for miraculous cures would not be accepted; by the twelfth issue, however, the lucrative medical narrative ads were accepted, with the publishers denying any responsibility for the reliability of the information within. The advertisements in the pages of the *British Apollo* cover a variety of topics and products, from the commonplace and boring, to the mysterious: A lady and her servant maid, identified as a "Blackamore," were taken to the Old Baily by convenance, but had left behind their little bandbox and if it was returned, it would earn a reward of ten shillings. In another ad, the enormous sum of five guineas was offered for a lost purse containing a ring with a "large Table-Diamond and six Small ones about it" along with another ring bearing a large ruby with eight diamonds, while the ad asking for assistance in returning a runaway servant, "James Armond in Green Livery lin'd with red," could only earn you two guineas.

According to his biographers, unlike Dunton who seems to have been quite proud of inventing the *Athenian Mercury*, Hill was only too happy to drop the *British Apollo* when a steadier source of income arose. While Dunton indeed had used the advertising space at the end of the *Athenian Mercury* to announce forthcoming titles to be had at his shop and to inquire after libraries for sale, Hill had used the periodical, especially in its first year, as a vehicle for promoting his own publications; Hill published several short poems without his name which were included in subsequent editions of Hill's works and, like Dunton, he used the advertisement section to draw attention and subscribers for his more ambitious literary projects. These included his expensive illustrated subscription volume, *A Full and Just Account of the Present State of the Ottoman Empire* (1709). Nevertheless, Hill quit the *British Apollo* without regret, and it ceased to publish shortly after this departure. As his *Oxford Dictionary of National Biography* entry states baldly, his new wife's substantial dowery "enabled

[100] Belcher, "The Sale and Distribution of the British Apollo," p. 89.

Hill to relinquish his journalistic hack work for the *British Apollo* . . . to embark on a career as a theatre impresario."[101]

## 3.2 Daniel Defoe and the Review: Capturing the Unsuspecting Reader with the Scandalous Club and the Little Review

In contrast to the man of letters fleeing from what was viewed as literary hackwork in connection with a successful periodical, Daniel Defoe, journalist, poet, essayist, and future novel writer devoted nearly a decade of his working life to a periodical in which he was the main contributor. As critics have observed, Daniel Defoe's *Review* (1704–1713), originally titled *A Weekly Review of the Affairs of France*, is in many ways a remarkable accomplishment, not the least of which is that for nine years, Defoe alone was responsible for the overwhelming majority of its content, estimated as writing three to five 2,000- to 2,500-word essays per week.[102] Its content has proved difficult for literary scholars to place or categorize. Christopher Flynn observes that it was "neither a newspaper, though it reported news, nor a periodical, though it contained essays."[103] As Flynn's digital edition of Defoe's journal was intended to highlight, the *Review* was involved in generating "new communities of readers," what Mary Poovey refers to as the "social imaginary."[104] Two spin-off publications from the *Review*, the *Mercure Scandale: Or Advice from the Scandalous Club*, which initially appeared at the end of each issue and was subsequently issued as in five monthly supplements starting in September 1704, and the *Little Review*, which appeared in a separate bi-weekly issue between June and August 1705. The existence of both spin-offs was not part of the original concept of the *Review*, but their existence, even if short-lived, demonstrate the potency of participatory culture established in earlier papers, whose authors actively invited readers to create its content.

Defoe's two supplemental publications emerged out of the primarily political opinion journal the *Review* (1704–1713) but, in contrast to it, were focused mostly on domestic topics. They both used the motif of a select "club" of sociable men with whom readers could interact through letters, although unlike Dunton, Defoe did not exert much effort in creating an actual group of

[101] Gerrard, "Hill, Aaron (1685–1750), writer and entrepreneur." *ODNB*.

[102] Cowan, "Daniel Defoe's Review and the Transformations of the English Periodical," p. 79. The original title of the *Review* was *Weekly Review of the Affairs of France*, changed to *Review of the Affairs of France* in 1705 when due to its popularity it began appearing three times a week. Subsequently, from 1706 it was called *Review of the State of the English Nation*, and in 1707 *Review of the State of the British Nation* after the union with Scotland.

[103] Flynn, "Defoe's Review: Textual Editing and New Media," p. 18.

[104] Flynn, 20; Poovey, "The Liberal Civil Subject and the Social in Eighteenth-Century British Moral Philosophy," p. 137.

responders, nor did he see it necessary to pretend that the "club" was anything but a fiction, and that at the heart of the supplements was the voice and opinion of a single individual – his.

The section which ended each issue of the early years of the *Review*, *Mercure Scandale: Or Advice from the Scandalous Club* (1704) was, as stated in the periodical, primarily intended for entertainment, a counterpoint to the weighty political topics of the main portion. Subsequently, in the bi-weekly *Little Review* (June–August 1705), Defoe again experimented with inviting readers to contact "Mr. Review" with their stories, gossip, and questions. Apparently, Defoe was overwhelmed by the volume and intensity of the *Review*'s readers and felt that it might overshadow the political contributions of the *Review*, for he discontinued both supplements, but not, however, before having them spun off for separate sale on their own and as collectibles to be bound in with the individual *Review* issues.

Initially, Defoe's *Review* focused on the state of affairs in England's chief international rival, France. As the *Review* continued, it enlarged its scope to include among other political topics the Union of England and Scotland, but he assured his readers in the second issue, February 16, 1704, the decision to include in each issue a concluding section devoted to *Mercure Scandale: Or, Advice from the Scandalous Club* was because it was an established feature of Parisian politics that he is merely translating for his English readers. In spite of its name, the function of the Scandalous Club was not to create scandals, and "the Business of this Society is to censure the Actions of Men, not Parties, and in particular, those Actions which are made publick so by the Authors, as to be, in their own Nature, an Appeal to the general Approbation."[105]

The first example from the Scandalous Club "records" is, tellingly, a man who announced the death of the Duke of Bavaria while he was still alive, and the club declared that it is "a scandalous Thing, That News-Writers shou'd kill Kings and Princes, and bring them to life again at pleasure." The larger issue here is fake news and the corruption of the relationship between the news writers and the general reading public: "the Club has had a great deal of trouble about the News-Writers, who have been continually brought before them for their ridiculous Stories, and imposing upon Mankind." The Scandalous Club's tone is a public spirited one, seeking to guard the unsuspecting reader from consuming misleading information by denouncing the rival purveyors of news, forming an alliance with its reader against unscrupulous news mongers.

[105] N. 2, February 26, 1704. All subsequent references will be to the John McVeigh edition of Defoe's *Review* and refer to the Volume and page numbers of that edition, not Defoe's original publications.

As Jean McBain has noted in her study of the eighteenth-century "emotional community" in print, Defoe altered the nature of this entertaining appendix over the course of the first few months of the periodical's existence. He shifted from the fiction of translating the fictional Parisian club's verdicts, which were mostly involved with castigating the veracity of the news reported in other periodicals, to answering queries from the English reading community.[106] As Defoe's biographer Maximillian Novak observes, "how many of the letters printed in the *Review* were composed or drastically revised by Defoe, we will never know . . . but that the vast majority were genuine there can be little doubt."[107] Defoe's contemporaries appear to have believed that the correspondence was real: John Dunton, observing the popularity of Defoe's new offering was not pleased by this change in the original format, and declaring that Defoe "has done me a sensible wrong, by interloping with my 'Question-Project,'" which undercut Dunton's own attempt to revive the brand with his *Monthly Oracle*.[108] Was it shrewd marketing by Defoe, or were English periodical readers exerting their influence over the type and format of periodical literature they wished to consume? While John Richetti has suggested Defoe was the prime instigator in altering the *Review*'s initial format to increase readership, McBain suggests that it was at the demands of his readers that drove Defoe and that "the Scandal Club became a participatory space through the impetus of readers rather than the discretion of Defoe."[109] In addition, a fictional identity for the responder began to emerge as well: "if Defoe created a kind of fictional character as 'as the Author of the Review' or 'Mr. Review,' it was more in these sections than in his writing on politics."[110]

The *Review*'s readers clearly had Dunton's Athenian publications in mind when assessing the new offering. Addressing "the Gentlemen of the Scandalous Club," one of the *Review*'s early letter writers observed, "I prefer your Club much before the Athenian Oracle."[111] Some early readers objected that the name of the group was confusing – were the members themselves scandalous? Defoe was at pains to reassure the concerned in the preamble to the Club's "Advice" from the September 5, 1704 issue, stating "the Design and Desire of Our Society being the Reforming, not Exposing the Vicious."[112] Likewise, in the "Introduction" to the first of the monthly "Supplementary Journal to the Advice

[106] McBain, "'Love, Marriages, Mistresses, and the Like,'" p. 71.

[107] Novak, *Daniel Defoe*, p. 214. [108] Dunton, *Life and Errors*, II: 423.

[109] Richetti, *Life of Daniel Defoe*, pp. 87, 89; McBain, "'Love, Marriages, Mistresses, and the Life,'" p. 71.

[110] Novak, *Daniel Defoe*, p. 215.

[111] *The Athenian Oracle* was Dunton's 1703 collection, reissued several times, of popular questions and answers that had been published in the old *Athenian Mercury*.

[112] *The Review*, I: 226.

from the Scandal Club," which appeared in September 1704, he opens by repeating that "this Society, having been design'd for examining and censuring Things Scandalous, and openly deserving Reproof" was not offering a sensational narrative in the sense that the popular *roman à clef* did, where readers were invited to identify the living persons in the narrative through thinly veiled allusions and clues, but instead seeking to identify types of corruption in public life.

Having settled this minor reader complaint, the writer admits that the Scandalous Club has strayed from its original purpose and that it has "insensibly been drawn into the difficult, nice, and unsatisfying Work of resolving Doubts, answering Questions, and deciding Controversies, Things absolutely remote and foreign to their first Design." Defoe asserts emphatically at another point that "answering Doubts, resolving Questions, and deciding Controversies, were as remote from his Thoughts, when he began this Paper, as making a Map of the World in the Moon."[113] The self-styled "Author" admits "the Hand that operates in this Work, being *allegorically* rather than *significantly* call'd a Society; may be for sundry Reasons uncapable of Performance in so vast a Variety as is like to come before him." In the process of switching between first person "I hope no Man will Censure me, for not knowing how to answer all the Questions Mankind can propose," to third person, "he humbly desires of the World, to send no Ensnaring Questions," the character of "Mr. Review" slowly emerges.[114]

While the *Review*, like the *Athenian Mercury* which preceded it, was in its format and publication practices a short, ephemeral publication, it seems clear that Defoe like Dunton from the start envisioned its transition into a collectable item, which readers could package and curate to suit their own personal tastes. Desiring his readers not to send "trifling things" to the paper which he cannot include, the Author states that "he hopes to Make the Collection worth a Man's keeping and worth Posterities Reading."[115] "Our Supplement," he explains, is "made for Want of Room in the Current Paper" to contain those things which are genuinely "Curious, any thing Experimental, either in History, in Politicks[,] in Physicks" and "the Author shall think himself and this Work, highly oblig'd to the Gentlemen who shall please to Communicate such things."

As a collectable, however, its initial readers apparently had some concerns that the Author directly addresses. Among his readers, the Author realizes that some "People that object against this part of the Work being too large," because they are concerned that it will be difficult to "bind up with the Collection of the Reviews, and yet necessary to go with them, because of the Connexion of Story and References from one to the other." In response, the Author declares that "it

[113] *The Review*, I: 390, 391. [114] *The Review*, I: 391. [115] *The Review*, I: 391–92.

shall be endeavour'd to order the Volumes of the Reviews to end some thing sooner, that the Addition of these [monthly] Supplements may not make them too bulky to bind together" and "it shall be endeavour'd to make them as Independent of one another as possible, that at last it may not be absurd to bind them apart." Against the objection that there is no audience for a Supplement, that "all the Coffee-houses, that take in your Penny Papers, will not be so ready to take the Supplement," it is noted that the Publisher "finds that the Sale of the Reviews differs much from the Common Method of such Publick Papers," and that "above one half of them are bought by Gentlemen, that lay them up to bind together in Volumes."[116] Perhaps sensitive to the perception of periodicals as being merely ephemeral adjuncts to drinking coffee for such readers who frequent public houses, the Author continues, "Gentlemen, and Men of Reading, Collect them, and as for such they were design'd, such will still approve it," and for the undiscerning casual reader, "they must take their own way."

Defoe highlights the didactic nature of this periodical in his explanations of why it is not a purely political or historical journal. The Scandalous Club and its *Supplement* are vital, in the Author's opinion, for the success of the mission of the *Review*, to attract and retain readers for the timely and more important historical and political topics contained in the paper. He describes the section as being "this honest Cheat," with the intention of balancing serious materials with entertaining, "to bring people to read with Delight."[117] Much as the civil war newsbook writers had asserted about using verses, Defoe reiterates in the "Introduction" to the first issue of the *Supplement*, "as the Merry Part of this Paper, [it] is not without its Uses," and he describes it as "an *Innocent Bait*, to bring some People in Love with the more substantial Part, and make them Read to their own profit and Instruction."

Defoe stopped publishing letters and the *Supplements* for the Scandal Club when "the Urgent Occasion of the Publick Affairs in the *Review* began also to Crowd it out" ("Introduction," the *Little Review*, Wednesday June 6, 1705). However, "the Number of Enquirers still increasing, and some very pressing to revive it," he consented to publish the *Little Review* separately on Wednesdays and Fridays in order to respond to readers' demands for a voice in the *Review*. As before in the Supplement, the fiction of "the Society" is continued with the majority of the letters addressed to "Gentlemen," or "Sir," but by the final issue of the *Little Review*, Number 21 August 15, 1705, the opening letter is addressed to "Mr. de Foe." The writer, who signs as "Your Sincere Friend," demands that the Author should "inform the World what Appellation the Society assumes;

[116] *The Review*, I: 392. [117] *The Review*, I: 393.

and whether it consists of a Number or a single Person; that they may know how to Address themselves properly to it, and not in the Plural if the Number be one, nor in the singular, if it be many." Defoe flatly admits that "we are one Person, sometimes Mr. *Review*, sometimes the *Scandal Club*, sometimes one single Body, sometimes a Body Corporate." Defoe concludes that "if you Write or Address your self to *Us*, *I* shall receive your Letter; or if you send to *Me*, *We* shall give you all the Satisfaction *I* can, for *We* are your *Friend* and *Servants, Nos Ego*."

As McBain noted, a large proportion of the letters answered by first the Scandal Club and then in the *Little Review* concern the control of emotions, but one feels that they are not like the friendly, sober exchanges found in the earlier periodicals. The next letter in this issue is in Latin, which is translated so "that the Ladyes, for whose Instruction they Write, may not be at the trouble to enquire the meaning." The young ladies reading it receive a strong warning as the letter comes from a young man, who having courted a young lady and reached an agreement, could not obtain the consent of her family. Rather than try to appease her family, it caused him to use "my best endeavours to get her to Bed to her without it; which I easily effected." Because, as he confesses "keeping a Secret being none of my Talent," the result is that "now her Father Threatens to go to Law with me." What should he do? First, the Club has some harsh words for the young woman: "a Woman that will take a Man's word in this Case, really ought to expect such Usage," and she has placed herself under his insults forever, and he will never believe that she will be chaste, as "Once a Whore and always so." The young man, on the other hand, "ought to be Punish'd for deluding the young Woman, but he ought to be hang'd for telling of it afterward." As for their advice, the Club urges that he should again ask her father for permission to marry her, "if she be Fool enough to have him," and should then take himself off and enlist in the army where perhaps he might be shot or, as an alternative, hang himself as a villain.

These are not the pious reflections of the Rev. Wesley in the *Athenian Mercury*, the chivalrous gallantry that characterizes the responses of the *Gentleman's Journal*, nor even the "young man about town" air of sophistication for which the *British Apollo* strove to appeal to its readers, but instead the voice of an individual moral authority. While Defoe successfully made use of the conventions of participatory culture initially to cultivate a subscribing readership, in the long run of the life of the *Review*, his focus was more on establishing and selling a trusted political and moral persona, himself. In doing so, he was operating in a different mode than what we will see with the successful contemporary periodicals by Richard Steele and Joseph Addison. In his growing resistance to sustaining a genuinely participatory culture, one based on the assumption of collegiality and sociable exchange between readers and writers of both sexes as seen in the earlier papers, Defoe foreshadows the practices of mid- and late-eighteenth-century periodicals.

## 4 Celebrity and the Changing Nature of Periodical Cultures: The *Tatler*, the *Spectator*, and their Rivals

> Individual interactions are valuable in almost any social media strategy. Why? Because people like to feel like they matter. . . . focus on answering individual questions, or replying to content created by individuals in your core following. If they feel listened to, valued, and respected, they'll probably become much more loyal to you – and encourage their friends and followers to follow you as well.
>
> –Jayson DeMers, "The 7 biggest secrets of social media influencers," X Business

> If it doesn't spread, it's dead.
>
> –Henry Jenkins, Sam Ford, and Joshua Green, *Spreadable Media*[118]

In contrast to Defoe's apparent rejection of a participatory sociable reading culture, the publications of Richard Steele and Joseph Addison and their friends embraced it and added a further dimension. Defoe's *Review* may have run longer, but the popularity of the *Tatler* and the *Spectator* among eighteenth-century readers was both rapid and enduring and they became a foundational part of the eighteenth-century literary canon. Rather than ceasing to appear because of lack of readers or financial support, both papers stopped their runs in part because of the simple exhaustion of their writers and editors with the demands of producing serial periodicals that appeared multiple times a week. Readers, on the other hand, were eager to continue to participate: sending their letters to Steele and Addison, many were clearly in hopes of themselves becoming part of this literary phenomenon, as one notes, "it is no Wonder if all Mankind endeavours to get somewhat into a paper which will always live."[119] For eighteenth-century readers of both sexes, the *Tatler* and the *Spectator* offered not only entertainment that was designed to be shared among family and friends, but also the chance to become members of the fictional world of Isaac Bickerstaff and Mr. Spectator.

As we saw in the opening section, for modern readers the *Tatler* and the *Spectator* are the model for periodical essays and their primary authors, Richard Steele and Joseph Addison, are the masters of the genre. "Of the hundreds of periodical essays which flourished in the eighteenth century the *Spectator* was one of the first in time, as it was also – in the opinion of competent judges – the most widely read and the best."[120] We do not think of these two

---

118 Jason DeMers, "The 7 biggest secrets"; Jenkins, Ford, and Green, *Spreadable Media*, p. 1; https://business.twitter.com/en/blog/secrets-of-social-media-influencers.html.

119 Richmond P. Bond, *New Letters to the Tatler and Spectator*, pp. 10–11.

120 *Spectator*, I, xiii.

papers as single half-sheet, double-columned, ephemeral publications (Figure 7) competing for advertisers, much less, as Rachael Scarborough King has argued, being "a branch of the news media."[121] Given the accumulated praise of generations for their literary accomplishment, it is very easy to lose sight of their original literary ecology. At the time of their first appearance, they were among a host of competitive rivals, all vying to entertain a very similar audience. During the five-year period 1709–1714 when the *Tatler* and the *Spectator* were being written, there were at least one hundred other competing periodicals, gazettes, and newspapers for reader to choose from.[122]

To a modern eye, the numbers of copies printed for the initial runs of the *Tatler* and the *Spectator* might not seem that impressive. Mr. Spectator proudly declares in issue #10 that 3,000 copies per issue were published of the paper, although Steele estimated that with the imposition of the stamp tax in 1712, the circulation was probably then cut in half.[123] Given the practice of one paper being shared among many readers in public spaces such as coffee houses and inns, however, it is difficult to say exactly how many readers they had based on numbers of copies. The *Tatler* had 330 issues in its two-year life (April 12, 1709 to January 2, 1711) while the *Spectator* appeared daily for sixteen months, (262 issues between March 1, 1711 and December 31, 1712), before changing to a thrice weekly distribution, concluding with issue 635 in December 1714. In the context of competing media of the day, however, these were impressive figures, with the *Tatler* having to bring in a second printing house to satisfy demand, and the *Spectator* from its start required an ever-increasing number of distribution outlets. What might be some of the reasons for their immediate popularity and what might have propelled these two publications from the coffee house and tea table into the English literary canon? Was it because they were so significantly different from the periodicals that preceded them and their contemporaries, or because they simply did what they did better?

The list of failed literary periodicals in the first and second decades of the eighteenth century is long. Samuel Phillips attempted to match the *Gentleman's Journal* with the *Poetical Courant* by offering only verse; much of, however, it appears was written by his colleagues in Oxford rather than the London theatre crowd. In an advertisement at the end, like Motteaux, he encourages "all Gentleman, Ladies &c who have any Original Copies of Verses, Heroical, Humourous, Galant, Satyrs, Odes, Epigrams, Riddles, Receipts, Songs, Prologues or Epilogues, &c. proper to insert in this Paper," to send them to

[121] King, "The *Gazette*, the *Tatler*, and the Making of the Periodical Essay: Form and Genre in Eighteenth-Century News," p. 48.

[122] See McLeod, *Graphical Directory* for this time span.

[123] See Donald F. Bond, "The First Printing of the *Spectator*," pp. 166–67.

Numb. 8

# The TATLER.

By *Isaac Bickerstaff* Esq;

*Quicquid agunt Homines nostri Farrago Libelli.*

From *Tuesday April* 26. to *Thursday April* 28. 1709.

*Will's Coffee-house, April* 26.

THE Play of *The London Cuckolds* was acted this Evening before a suitable Audience, who were extremely well diverted with that Heap of Vice and Absurdity. The Indignation which *Eugenio*, who is a Gentleman of a just Tast, has, upon Occasion of seeing Human Nature fall so low in their Delights, made him, I thought, expatiate upon the Mention of this Play very agreeably. Of all Men living, said he, I pity Players, (who must be Men of good Understanding to be capable of being such) that they are oblig'd to repeat and assume proper Gestures for representing Things, of which their Reason must be asham'd, and which they must disdain their Audience for approving. The Amendment of these low Gratifications is only to be made by People of Condition, by encouraging the Presentation of the Noble Characters drawn by *Shakespear* and others, from whence it is impossible to return without strong Impressions of Honour and Humanity. On these Occasions, Distress is laid before us, with all its Causes and Consequences, and our Resentment plac'd according to the Merit of the Persons afflicted. Were *Drama's* of this Nature more acceptable to the Tast of the Town, Men who have Genius would bend their Studies to excel in 'em. How forcible an Effect this would have on our Minds, one needs no more than to observe how strongly we are touch'd by meer Pictures. Who can see *Le Brun's* Picture of the Battle of *Porus*, without entring into the Character of that fierce gallant Man, and being accordingly spur'd to an Emulation of his Constancy and Courage? When he is falling with his Wound, the Features are at the same Time very terrible and languishing; and there is such a stern Faintness diffus'd through all his Look, as is apt to move a kind of Horrour, as well as Pity, in the Beholder. This, I say, is an Effect wrought by meer Lights and Shades; consider farther a Representation made by Words only, as in an Account giv'n by a good Writer: *Cataline* in *Salust* makes just such a Figure, as *Porus* by *Le Brun*. It is said of him, Catalina *vero longe a suis inter Hostium Cadavera repertus est; paululum etiam spirans, ferocemque Animi quam vivus habuerat in Vultu retinens.* 'Cataline was found kill'd far from his own 'Men among the dead Bodies of the Enemy: He 'seem'd still to breath, and still retain'd in his Face 'the same Fierceness he had when he was living. You have in that one Sentence a lively Impression of his whole Life and Actions. What I would insinuate from all this, is, that if the Painter and the Historian can do thus much in Colours and Language, what may not be perform'd by an excellent Poet? When the Character he draws is presented by the Person, the Manner, the Look, and the Motion of an accomplish'd Player: If a Thing painted or related can irresistibly enter our Hearts, what may not be brought to pass by seeing generous Things perform'd before our Eyes? *Eugenio* ended his Chat, by recommending the apt Use of a Theatre, as the most agreeable and easie Method of making a Polite and Moral Gentry, which would end in rendring the rest of the People regular in their Behaviour, and ambitious of laudable Undertakings.

*St. James's Coffee-house, April* 27.

Letters from *Naples* of the 9th Instant, *N. S.* advise, That Cardinal *Grimani* had order'd the Regiment commanded by General *Pate* to march towards *Final*, in order to embark for *Catalonia*, whither also a Thousand Horse are to be transported from *Sardinia*, besides the Troops which come from the *Milanese*. An *English* Man of War has taken Two Prizes, one a Vessel of *Malta*, the other of *Genoa*, both laden with Goods of the Enemy. They write from *Florence* of the 13th, That his Majesty of *Denmark* had receiv'd a Courier from the *Hague*, with an Account of some Matters relating to the Treaty of a Peace; upon which he declar'd, that he thought it necessary to hasten to his own Dominions.

Letters from *Swisserland* inform us, That the Effects of the great Scarcity of Corn in *France* were felt at *Geneva*; the Magistrates of which City had appointed Deputies to treat with the Cantons of *Bern* and *Zurich*, for Leave to buy up such Quantities of Grain within their Territories as should be thought necessary. The Protestants of *Tockenbourg* are still in Arms about the Convent of St. *John*, and have declar'd, That they will not lay them down, till they shall have sufficient Security from the Roman Catholicks, that they shall live unmolested in the Exercise of their Religion. In the mean Time the Deputies of *Bern* and *Tockenbourg* have frequent Conferences at *Zurich*, with the Regency of that Canton, to find out Methods for the quieting these Disorders.

Letters from the *Hague* of the 3d of *May* advise, That the President *Rouille*, after his last Conference with the Deputies of the States, had retir'd to *Bodegrave*, five Miles off of *Worden*, and expected the Return of a Courier from *France*, with new Instructions, on the 4th. It is said, if his Answer from the *French* Court shall not prove Satisfactory, he will be desired to withdraw out of these Parts. In the mean time it is also reported, That his Equipage, as an Ambassador on this great Occasion, is actually on the March towards him. They write from *Flanders*, That the great Convoy of Provisions, which set out from *Ghent*, is safely arriv'd at *Lisle*. Those Advices add, That the Enemy had assembled near *Tournay* a considerable Body of Troops drawn out of the neighbouring Garisons. Their High Mightinesses having sent Orders to their Ministers at *Hamburgh* and *Dantzick*, to engage the Magistrates of those Cities to forbid the Sale of Corn to the

7.5 cm (3 in)

**Figure 7.** *The Tatler*, no. 8 (1709). Private collection, M. J. M. Ezell.

Goddard's Coffee house or to the publisher Benjamin Bragg and the author "will faithfully Insert 'em, and carefully Correct 'em."[124] The *Poetical Courant*, however, managed only twenty-three issues between January and June 1706. *The Muses Mercury*, a monthly periodical publishing contemporary poetry, including some by Dryden and in which Motteaux himself published verse translations, lasted only a year after it first appeared in 1707. Likewise, a periodical publishing only short fictions, the *Records of Love, Or Weekly Amusements for the Fair*, managed only twelve issues before expiring in the spring of 1710, although its first quarter was republished as a compact volume. As a periodical paper, however, the *Records of Love* appears to have misjudged the tastes of its readers and its stories, one per issue, "guaranteed to offend neither Political or moral sensibilities" did not last.[125]

Despite the large number of choices being offered readers, in the eyes of contemporaries such as John Gay, the state of periodicals in 1711, when the *Tatler* had ceased publication and the *Spectator* yet to start, was grim. According to Gay, the *Monthly Philosophical Transactions* were no longer being read, and its author ended up in prison for debt; one of Addison's associates, the translator's John Ozell's *Monthly Amusement* is described by Gay as only giving accounts of "some French Novel or Play indifferently taken Notion of"; Defoe's *Review* is "quite exhausted, and grown so very Contemptible" that the writer cannot persuade any of the other pamphlet writers to engage in a controversy with him. The political periodicals such as L'Estrange's the *Observator* and Swift's the *Examiner* are too embroiled in party politics, Gay asserts, to be entertaining.[126] But the *Tatler* and subsequently the *Spectator* appear to have found a ready and appreciative audience, who had been well-prepared to receive them by their predecessors.

As we shall see, both the *Tatler* and the *Spectator* employed many of the familiar and successful strategies of the sociable periodicals from the 1690s and early 1700s to create a community of readers who would be loyal to the papers. They encouraged their readers to create part of the content through correspondence; they offered an attractive group of characters representing a range of English society and family roles, whose stories and opinions appealed to a variety of readers; and, I will argue, they successfully created a sense of the

---

[124] The *Poetical Courant*, January 26, 1706.

[125] McLeod, *A graphical directory of English newspapers and periodicals, 1702–1714*, p. 46. It is notable that one of his advertisers appears to have been his mother, Mary Carey, who ran a boarding school: It is described in the ad as educating "young Gentlewomen" in the "Inditing of Letters . . . also that Graceful Accomplishment of Reading the most difficult *English* Authors with the greatest ease and exactness," who might have seemed the perfect target audience. The *Record of Love* (1710), p. 175.

[126] Gay, *The Present State of Wit* (1711), pp. 6–10.

reader being part of a familiar, insider relationship with the writers behind narrators, or the eidolons. Instead of the shadow figure of "P.M." in the *Gentleman's Journal* or the anonymous Athenian Society and *British Apollo*'s group of learned men, the *Tatler* and the *Spectator* offered readers the chance to connect not only to their own social groups but also that of the London-based celebrity writer.

Some of the papers' success rests on the familiarity readers would have with its format as serial publications. Initially, like the other miscellany format periodicals, the *Tatler* offered topical news so that "*Persons of strong Zeal and weak Intellects . . . may be instructed, after their Reading*, what to think" (#1, April 12, 1709; 1:15). Ashley Marshall has commented that "anyone familiar with the critical consensus on *The Tatler* must be somewhat surprised by the degree to which the early numbers are saturated by news reportage" and how initially it resembled the *Review* more than the *Spectator*.[127] As we shall see, unlike their predecessors, the content of the *Tatler* evolved, starting in this miscellany mode but the news aspect quickly faded in importance as its narrator Isaac Bickerstaff's "lucubrations" on contemporary culture and responses to readers commanded more space and more attention from the readers.

Like their predecessors, these papers, too, relied more and more on reader participation to supply content. Like Defoe's *Review*, the *Tatler* did not originally start out by soliciting letters or poetry, but over time, as Donald F. Bond suggests, Steele's "practice of printing letters from readers certainly aided in making the paper popular and established further rapport between editor and subscribers."[128] In issue #7, April 26, 1709, Bickerstaff makes a direct appeal to his readers: He asks that those willing to "transmit to me the Occurrences you meet with relating to your Amours, or any other Subject within the Rules by which I have proposed to walk" to send them by the now familiar Penny Post to him at Mr. Morphew's, the printer.[129] He urges gentlemen and ladies to communicate the "Grief or Joy of their Soul," adding that without such assistance, "I have not a Month's Wit more." Mr. Spectator, having learned the lessons from the changing format of the *Tatler*, made his appeal for readers' correspondence in the first issue, giving the address of his printer, Samuel Buckley in Little Britain. Issue #8 offers two letters with contrasting views on masquerades, concluding with Mr. Spectator's decision to visit the next London masquerade himself "in the same Habit I wore at *Grand Cairo*."[130] Did readers also wish to attend that masquerade and speculate who there was Mr. Spectator?

[127] *Tatler*, I: 15; Marshall, *Political Journalism in London*, p. 160. [128] *Tatler*, I, xx.
[129] *Tatler*, I: 63. [130] *Spectator*, I: 38.

The success of such petitions to readers is reflected not only in the ones reproduced in the periodicals but also in the subsequent merchandising of materials associated with them. In 1725, *Original and Genuine Letters Sent to the Tatler and Spectator During the Time those Works were publishing. None of which have been before Printed* was printed by Charles Lillie. Towards the end of his life, Steele permitted the perfumer Lillie to print unpublished letters sent to Bickerstaff and Mr. Spectator that were not "contrary to religion or good manners," and whose contents would not offend an individual or a family. Lillie had himself written to *Tatler* in #92, November 10, 1709, to ask Mr. Bickerstaff to "beg the Favour of being advantageously exposed in your Paper, chief for the Reputation of Snuff"; he subsequently enjoyed the custom of "several of my gentle Readers," although Bickerstaff denies in #96, November 19, 1709 that they are business partners (*Tatler*, 2: 78; 98). Lillie's shop on the Strand, along with Morphew's print shop, received readers' letters to Bickerstaffe, a role Lillie continued for the *Spectator.*[131]

Such was its appeal, Lillie's eight-hundred-page, two-volume collection was published by subscription, with initial purchasers ranging from the Duke and Duchess of Grafton who put down for six copies between them, to "Mr Daniel De Foe" and "Daniel De Foe junior," and the poet Ambrose Philips, to the unknown Elizabeth and Bersheba Mead, and "Mr. Lewis Lacoude, Merchant. For two Books." As Lillie notes in his "Preface," the sheer number of letters in the volumes is evidence of "how Laudable and beneficial a work the Tatlers and Spectators were, when they set all the writing world amongst us to work, each with a view to amend their neighbor." In the twentieth-century two more caches of unpublished letters that had been preserved and endorsed by Steele were found.[132] These ninety-six letters clearly are genuine as they are endorsed by Steele, not only with information about their topic but also how they were delivered, whether by Penny Post or its short-lived rival, the Half-Penny Post.

Even the letters which were not used in the *Tatler* or the *Spectator* reveal to us how contemporary readers thought about the two periodicals, creating an ongoing conversations between readers and the authors. The writers of the unpublished letters clearly enjoyed role playing, inventing names and identities for themselves, such as "J. Dapper," "Tom. Tell-Troth," "R. Middle-Thought," "Mary Spinster," and "Antigamus" who writes from the very real Pall-mall Coffee House, as well as more familiar coterie style names such as "Lydia," "Sylvia," and "Philis." Mimicking Bickerstaff and Mr. Spectator, these

[131] "Preface," *Original and Genuine Letters*, n.p.

[132] Richmond P. Bond, *New Letters to the Tatler and Spectator*, pp. 10–11.

correspondents often identify from whence they are writing, ranging from "my closet" to "Jacob's Coffee house behind the Exchange."

In Letter #1 of *Original and Genuine Letters*, "Ric. Wildair" sends a copy of a poem sent to him to Mr. Spectator, signing himself "your humble admirer, (not only now you are a mute, but when you was a tatler" (1:1). The writers of Letter #37 addressed to Mr. Spectator allude to an issue of the *Tatler*: "You having formerly (though in a different capacity) given us expectation of an account of a piece of painting," a reference a to *Tatler* #209 when Bickerstaff suggested a topic for a historical piece representing Alexander the Great. The topic was not taken up in subsequent issues, but the letter writers "assure you [it] will be very acceptable" even now to his readers at the Grecian Coffee House (I: 93). The communal aspect of reading the *Tatler* and the *Spectator* is highlighted by another reader comments to Mr. Spectator that "every one of your papers is a sermon, which is handed about to greater numbers of readers than most sermons . . . that were ever printed" (II: 173).

In Letter #4, "Isabella Thoughtful" writes to Mr. Bickerstaff that she has just returned from an "entertainment" where the ladies applauded the *Tatler* #67 (which contained thoughts on women wearing beauty patches) and "we all toasted you in tea" (1:6). Likewise in #136, "J. Dapper" informs Mr. Spectator that he has just left "the most agreeable tea-table in the world, . . . [where] the Spectator never failed of being a welcome guest" (II: 349). The persons there agreed with Mr. Spectator's observations on punning in issue #504 as being fashionable but not amusing and there was a "warm debate" over an anecdote illustrating the practice of "biting" or misleading a credulous hearer with a fictitious tale.

Whether or not all the letters in Lillie's printed collection were genuine, they consistently represent the reading of the *Tatler* and *Spectator* papers as being part of a participatory social media event, involving multiple readers discussing and circulating their contents. Nicola Parsons' analysis of the function of gossip as a key source of content for the *Tatler* notes the relish with which readers discussed the real-life identities of characters in the essays and the "convivial reading and discussion the paper stimulated," an aspect clearly seen in the unpublished letters.[133] Parsons records the example of a Lady Marow advising her daughter she should be reading the *Tatler,* for "all the town are full of the *Tatler*, which I hope you have to prepare you for discourse, for no visit is made that I hear of but Mr Bickerstaff is mentioned."[134]

In addition to providing their readers with real addresses and real people to which they could send their letters to be read by Bickerstaff and Mr. Spectator,

[133] Parsons, *Reading Gossip*, p. 98. [134] Parsons, *Reading Gossip*, p. 98.

the two papers reinforced the sense of community through other strategies. Readers became acquainted with Bickerstaff's friends and family, including his sister Jenny, more of whom later, as well as real individuals such as the printers and Charles Lilli who served as a living point of connection between readers and the worlds of Mr. Bickerstaff and Mr. Spectator. Both featured the stories of a collection of characters that were representative of the readership itself. The Club, introduced in the second issue of the *Spectator*, introduced readers to a collection of personalities with whom to identify, from the charming eccentric bachelor Sir Roger de Coverley, the modern merchant Sir Andrew Freeport, the military man Captain Sentry, and the man about town, Will Honeycomb.

The blending of fictional characters with real life London settings and people created for the original readers a sense that one might encounter personalities they knew from the papers in person. By heading the various sections of the papers as arising from specific public locations, whether Will's Coffee House or the Exchange, the reader is given a sense that they, too, if they were in London, might be present at the events and conversations being described by Bickerstaff and Mr. Spectator. As with the *Gentleman's Journal* discussed before, this helps to create a sense for the reader that they, too, might become contributors, not just consumers. As Iona Italia commented on the *Spectator*, "knowing the editor's haunts invited readers to guess at his real identity, … or recognize the pen-portraits of friends and acquaintance. Frequenting the same coffee-houses as the editor made them part of the extended club formed by the periodical's readers."[135]

The success of both the *Tatler* and the *Spectator* in creating these artificial communities where readers are invited to interact with the central characters, I would argue, make the *Tatler* and the *Spectator* stronger literary "brands" than many of the rival periodicals; like bloggers today are encouraged to do, they offered a lifestyle appealing to their target audience. They likewise created a more successful first-person narrators, or eidolons, ones which combined idealized characteristics designed to appeal to an eighteenth-century reader and to establish an authoritative voice, and ones which readers, through their careful reading, might well be able to find out the names of the real authors behind them.

The "eidolon," as defined in the *Oxford English Dictionary* is "a character in a literary work who represents or embodies the author," "a fictional authorial or editorial persona adopted by the writer or writers." It is considered by recent critics to be a defining characteristic of the eighteenth-century English periodical, "the eponymous authorial persona … is the genre's most characteristic formal feature," according to Osell; Manushag N. Powell suggests that "the eidolon makes the invisible visible, giving solid print form to the relationship

[135] Italia, *Rise of Literary Journalism*, p. 79.

between reader and author, manifesting, in a profitable and creative way, the reader's desire to 'see' authorship itself."[136] While Osell interprets the periodical eidolon as being "basically transparent, meant to point to the author rather than substitute for or shield him or her," Powell in contrast declares that the eidolon is a performative, socialized self-identity, a "public piece of writing" designed in part both to entice and satisfy the reader's desire to have a relationship with the author.[137]

This artificial authorial identity, in Powell's argument, is a crucial one to distinguish the periodical writer from the anonymous gazetteer or a Grub Street hack writer for hire. As she notes, the eidolons of eighteenth-century periodicals typically are "at pains to declare, generally falsely, the lack of economic interest among their reasons for publication: Isaac Bickerstaff in the *Tatler*, and Mr. Spectator in the *Spectator* are gentlemen of leisure and reflection."[138] It is important to note here that "Bickerstaff" and "Mr. Spectator" did not function like pseudonyms such as Mary Ann Evans's George Eliot, intended to hide the author's name and gender, but were characters themselves that become merged with the writer's public image. As Carla L. Peterson notes, Bickerstaff and Mr. Spectator were "not meant to confer anonymity, functioning instead as an open secret. ... the eidolon was never identical to the author but rather the author and his fictional representation simultaneously, thus offering readers a carefully constituted public image."[139] As Powell notes, in general, early eighteenth-century eidolons were meant to be "puzzles for the reader to cipher through."[140]

Readers in the first part of the eighteenth century had long been accustomed to deciphering the identities of real people presented in fictional garb, especially when embedded in satires. Whether it was interpreting the exotic romance *Hattigé* as being about Charles II and his mistress the Duchess of Cleveland, or speculating on the identities of Queen Anne's courtiers in the scandalous *roman á clef* by Delarivier Manley, *Secret Memoirs and Manners ... the New Atalantis* (1709), early eighteenth-century readers were conditioned to be aware of characters' resemblances to real persons.[141] The *Tatler* regaled the reader with veiled accounts of actual scandals, which its readers were apparently quick to decipher: Peter Wentworth writing to his brother identifies the character of "Africanus," as being Sir Scipio Hill (I: 265 n.4), while Abigail Harley

[136] Osell, *Ghost Writer*, p. ii; Powell, *Performing Authorship*, p. 23.

[137] Powell, *Performing*, pp. 26–27. [138] Powell, *Performing*, pp. 31, 32.

[139] Peterson, "Mapping Taste," p. 695. [140] Powell, *Performing*, pp. 26, 27.

[141] See Loveman, *Reading Fictions, 1660–1740* and Carnell, "Slipping from Secret History to Novel."

deciphered the character of Cynthio in first issue for her aunt as being Lord Hinchinbrooke who in the throes of love appeared drunk at a playhouse.[142]

"Isaac Bickerstaff" was already established as a vehicle for social critique through Jonathan Swift's use of it in satirizing the popular astrologer and Whig propagandist John Patridge in 1708; the name was subsequently adopted by multiple Tory authors in 1710 writing about the celebrity trial of Dr. Sacheverell.[143] The real "authors" behind the eidolons of Isaac Bickerstaff (both in the case of Swift and later the *Tatler*) and Mr. Spectator were widely discussed, although, of course, it is impossible to say how many or how quickly readers guessed correctly. Bond records that Peter Wentworth sent two issues of the *Tatler* to his brother in Berlin in early May 1709, shortly after the paper began appearing: "Three of the authors are guest [guessed] at, viz. Swift, that writ the tale of the tub, Yalden, fellow of Magdilin [*sic*] College, Oxford, and Steel, the Gazzetier," scoring a two out of three.[144] Steele states in the final issue of the *Tatler*, #271, January 2, 1711, not quite two years after the first paper appeared, that the reason he is stopping is because he is now so widely known to be the author. He starts pragmatically by noting that his printers inform him that there are enough issues to make up the fourth volume; he concludes that he has "nothing further to say to the World, under the Character of *Isaac Bickerstaff.* This Work has indeed for some Time been disagreeable to me, and the Purpose of it wholly lost by my being so long understood as the Author."[145]

Osell observes that "virtually all canonical essay periodicals are identified with particular authors, especially authors whose literary success extended to other genres."[146] This is not the way in which the authors and editors of the periodicals we examined in previous sections functioned. In contrast with the *Athenian Mercury* and the *Gentleman's Journal* (especially in their original single-sheet and pamphlet formats), the fictions which framed their contents, a nameless society of learned gentlemen and a chatty London correspondent who moved in fashionable literary circles, served to veil the commercial literary

[142] Parsons, *Reading Gossip*, p. 97.

[143] McTague, "Patridge, Pittis, and Jonathan Swift," p. 98, n.9.

[144] Quoted by Bond, *Tatler*, I: xiii. The Wentworth family were enthusiastic readers of the *Tatler* and the *Spectator*, frequently commenting on its contents and sharing issues. *Wentworth Papers 1705–1739*, ed. Cartwright (1883).

[145] *Tatler*, 3: 362. It is also significant the extent to which Steele, while acknowledging the assistance of others, by the end of his life is firmly claiming the *Tatler* and the Bickerstaffe "brand" as his. Steele was irritated that Jacob Tonson intended to include the essays in the *Tatler* by Addison in his edition of Addison's works: "I apprehend certain Persons desire to separate the works of Mr. Addison from mine in a Book called the Tatler. Be pleased to observe that I insist I payd Mr. Addison for what he writ under that title," Steele wrote in 1719, a month after Addison's death, apparently feeling that the entirety of the *Tatler* was his and his family's literary property.

[146] Osell, *Ghost Writer*, p. 151.

NUMB. LXXXIX.

# The SPECTATOR.

——————*Petite hinc Juveneſque ſeneſque*
*Finem animo certum, miſeriſque viatica canis.*
*Cras hoc fiet. Idem cras fiet. Quid? quaſi magnum*
*Nempe diem donas; ſed cum lux altera venit,*
*Jam cras heſternum conſumpſimus; ecce aliud cras*
*Egerit hos annos, & ſemper paulum erit ultra.*
*Nam quamvis prope te, quamvis temone ſub uno*
*Vertentem ſeſe fruſtra ſectabere canthum.* Per.

*Tueſday, June* 12. 1711.

AS my Correſpondents, upon the Subject of Love, are very numerous, it is my Deſign, if poſſible, to range them under ſeveral Heads, and addreſs my ſelf to them at different Times. The firſt Branch of them, to whoſe Service I ſhall Dedicate this Paper, are thoſe that have to do with Women of Dilatory Tempers, who are for ſpinning out the Time of Courtſhip to an immoderate Length without being able either to cloſe with their Lovers, or to diſmiſs them. I have many Letters by me filled with Complaints againſt this ſort of Women. In one of them no leſs a Man than a Brother of the Coiff tells me, that he began his Suit *Viceſſimo nono Caroli ſecundi*, before he had been a Twelve-month at the *Temple*; that he proſecuted it for many Years after he was called to the Bar; that at preſent he is a Serjeant at Law; and notwithſtanding he hoped that Matters would have been long ſince brought to an iſſue, the Fair One ſtill *Demurrs*. I am ſo well pleaſed with this Gentleman's Phraſe, that I ſhall diſtinguiſh this Sect of Women by the Title of *Demurrers*. I find by another Letter from one who calls himſelf *Thirſis*, that his Miſtreſs has been Demurring above theſe ſeven Years. But among all my Plaintiffs of this nature, I moſt pity the unfortunate *Philander*, a Man of a conſtant Paſſion and plentiful Fortune, who ſets forth that the timorous and irreſolute *Sylvia* has demurred till ſhe is paſt Child-bearing. *Strephon* appears by his Letter to be a very Cholerick Lover, and irrevocably ſmitten with one that demurrs out of Self-intereſt. He tells me, with great Paſſion, that ſhe has bubbled him out of his Youth; that ſhe has drilled him on to Five and Fifty, and that he verily believes ſhe will drop him in his old Age, if ſhe can find her account in another. I ſhall conclude this Narrative with a Letter from Honeſt SAM. HOPEWELL, a very pleaſant Fellow, who it ſeems has, at laſt, married a *Demurrer*. I muſt only premiſe, that SAM. who is a very good Bottle-Companion, has been the Diverſion of his Friends, upon account of his Paſſion, ever ſince the Year One thouſand Six hundred and Eighty one.

*Dear Sir,*

'YOU know very well my Paſſion for Mrs. *Martha*, and what a Dance ſhe has led me: She took me out at the Age of Two and Twenty, and dodged with me above Thirty Years. I have loved her till ſhe is grown as Grey as a Cat, and am with much ado become the Maſter of her Perſon, ſuch as it is at preſent. She is however, in my Eye, a very charming old Woman. We often lament that we did not marry ſooner, but ſhe has no Body to blame for it but her ſelf. You know very well that ſhe would never think of me whilſt ſhe had a Tooth in her Head. I have put the Date of my Paſſion (*Anno Amoris Trigeſimo primo*) inſtead of a Poſie on my Wedding Ring. I expect you ſhould ſend me a Congratulatory Letter; or, if you pleaſe, an *Epithalamium* upon this occaſion.

*Mrs.* Martha'*s and*

*Yours Eternally,*

SAM. HOPEWELL.

In order to baniſh an Evil out of the World, that does not only produce great Uneaſineſs to private Perſons, but has alſo a very bad Influence on the Publick, I ſhall endeavour to ſhow the Folly of *Demurrage*, from two or three Reflections, which I earneſtly recommend to the Thoughts of my Fair Readers.

Firſt of all I would have them ſeriouſly think on the Shortneſs of their Time. Life is not long enough for a Coquet to play all her Tricks in. A timorous Woman drops into her Grave before ſhe has done deliberating Were the Age of Man the ſame that it was before the Flood, a Lady might ſacrifice half a Century to a Scruple, and be two or three Ages in demurring. Had ſhe Nine Hundred Years good, ſhe might hold out to the Converſion of the *Jews*, before ſhe thought fit to be prevailed upon. But, alas! ſhe ought to play her Part in haſte, when ſhe conſiders that ſhe

7.5 cm (3 in)

**Figure 8.** *The Spectator*, no. 89 (1711). Private collection, M. J. M. Ezell.

entrepreneurship which was propelling the creation of the journal and its contents. As I have argued before, the fictional speaker(s) in each of these periodicals was not a stand-in for the author, but a cloaking device which wrapped the commercial aspects of the publication in the refined garb of familiar coterie, social authorship practices.[147] One cannot imagine, for example, that it would have improved the circulation of the *Athenian Mercury* if Dunton had explained that the "society" was himself and his brother-in-law – it was imperative that the identities of the society be left pleasingly ambiguous, or as critics such as Berry and Powell have argued, that the *Athenian Mercury* readers remain "duped" into believing that "the society was both more educated and more specialized than in reality."[148] The author of the *British Apollo* and his society of learned gentlemen was vigorously attacked in the *Female Tatler*, but his identity stayed resolutely behind the mask of the learned society – there was no "Mr. Apollo."

In contrast, as Mr. Spectator observed in the first issue of the paper, "a Reader seldom peruses a Book with Pleasure 'till he knows whether the Writers of it be a black or a fair Man, of mild or cholerick Disposition, Married or a Batchelor, with other Particulars of the like nature, that conduce very much to the right Understanding of an Author."[149] The opening issues of the *Spectator* are designed to provide these fictional biographies of not only the speaker, but also of his friends. Mr. Spectator firmly establishes about himself that "where-ever I see a Cluster of People I always mix with them, tho' I never open my Lips but in my own Club," and famously "I live in the World, rather as a Spectator of Mankind, than as one of the Species." Mr. Spectator concludes this issue by stating that he chooses not to reveal "my Name, my Age, and my Lodgings," even though he realizes that such personal details "might tend very much to the Embellishment of my Paper"; he does, however, leave the possibility open that in future issues, along with the details of his "Complexion and Dress," that "I may make Discoveries of both in the Progress of the Work I have undertaken."[150]

Addison is demonstrating his awareness that readers would very much like to know more personal details about Mr. Spectator's appearance and temperament, and in fact that including such personal details about the author are now, as with social media platforms today, an important element being an "author" and in creating and sustaining an audience. By 1709 when the *Tatler* first appeared, Richard Steele was well-known to the reading public (Figure 9) as the author of *The Christian Hero*, which went through twenty editions, as well as having

[147] See Ezell, "*The Gentleman's Journal* and the Commercialization of Restoration Coterie Literary Practices."
[148] Berry, *Gender Society and Print Culture*, p.20; Powell, *Performing Authorship*, p. 33.
[149] *Spectator*, I: 1. [150] *Spectator*, I: 5–6.

**Figure 9.** Mr. Richard Steele (1712) by and sold by John Smith, after Jonathan Richardson mezzotint, 1713 (1712). NPG D42159. © National Portrait Gallery, London.

produced three plays and serving as the editor of the *London Gazette*. Both Addison and Steele were members of the powerful, widely networked Whig Kit Kat club; Addison had carved out success in the literary realm with the publication of his poem *The Campaign* celebrating the victories of the Duke of Marlborough, and his libretto for the opera *Rosamond*, dedicated to the Duchess of Marlborough, and had been elected to Parliament.[151] Continuing Osell's observation that the authorship of the *Tatler* and the *Spectator* was soon an open secret to its readers, I suggest that the popularity of these eidolons as linked to known, public individuals is part of the contemporary phenomenon of the invention of a celebrity media culture, also based on the creation of a type of artificial public intimacy between writer and reader, again a defining characteristic of modern successful social media authors, generating fans and followers.

Literary and cultural critics such as Joseph Roach and Felicity Nussbaum have attributed origins of many of the techniques of celebrity to Restoration actresses such as Nell Gwynn, Elizabeth Barry, and Kitty Clive, with their

[151] See Winton, "Steele, Sir Richard (bap. 1672, d. 1729), writer and politician," *ODNB*; Rogers, "Addison, Joseph (1672–1719), writer and politician," *ODNB*.

strategic deployment of elements of their personal, private lives merging with their professional performances, which I have argued was also manifest in the marketing of women writers such as Aphra Behn and Susanna Centlivre.[152] The creation of a celebrity figure, whether actor or writer, in the early eighteenth century involved the strategic deployment of several media, functioning like today's transmedia, to present, circulate, and sell to the eager public the celebrity's image as well as letters or personal writings. This helps to create an artificial sense of intimacy with the admired figure and a desire to gain even more "insider" knowledge about them on the part of their fans. Celebrity went hand in hand with the marketing of a figure's personal artifacts such as printed portraits or letters, which is different from that associated with collecting the loose papers of earlier periodicals in nice bindings with an index.[153] While Addison and Steele may have lacked the glamor of the actresses, they were both public men, known for their literary abilities as well as their political writing, and their associations with the Kit Kat club.

Unlike the notoriety strategically wielded by celebrity actresses, however, as Kathryn Shevelow noted, the established tone of the eighteenth-century eidolon in periodical culture was that of a moral authority.[154] This also highlights the public image of the speaker/ author as a figure with public authority to comment on social mores. While periodicals such as the *Philosophical Transactions* and the *Athenian Mercury* entertained their readers on a wide range knowledge on various topics, as we have seen, Defoe had highlighted in the *Review* the moral and ethical function of his two supplements to the *Review*, in particular the opinions of the Scandalous Club. The *Tatler* increasingly offered essays devoted to general social critique and news, and the eidolon of Isaac Bickerstaff emerged as that acceptable voice of authority. As Steele explained in his final issue, his sole intention was "to recommend Truth, Innocence, Honour, and Virtue, as the chief Ornaments of Life" through censoring examples of lamentable "fashionable Vices." He describes Bickerstaff as "an old Man, a Philosopher, an Humorist, an Astrologer, and a Censor," whose "Severity of Manners," would counter-balance Richard Steele the writer's widely known less than perfect moral life: Mr. Bickerstaff was thus able to criticize contemporary individuals and events "with a Freedom of Spirit that

[152] See Roach, *It*, chapter one; Nussbaum, "Actresses and the Economics of Celebrity, 1700–1800" and *Rival Queens*; and Ezell, "Penny Post."

[153] See for example the vogue for publishing letters by famous writers as seen in the publisher Samuel Briscoe's multivolume sets of *Familiar letters of love, gallantry, and several other occasions* (1718–1724).

[154] Shevelow, "Re-Writing the Moral Essay."

would have lost both its Beauty and Efficacy, had it been pretended to by Mr. *Steele*."[155]

Likewise, Mr. Spectator declared in #10, March 12, 1711 that having heard from his publisher that some three thousand copies are distributed daily, and with "Twenty Readers to every Paper, which I look upon as a modest Computation," that in pursuit of his goal of making "their Instruction agreeable, and their Diversion useful," he shall "endeavour to enliven Morality with Wit, and to temper Wit with Morality."[156] "I shall be ambitious," he concludes, "to have it said of me, that I have brought Philosophy out of Closets and Libraries, Schools and Colleges, to dwell in Clubs and Assemblies, at Tea-Tables, and in Coffee-Houses." Information itself, whether scientific, historical, theological, or topical news was not the reason for these periodicals to come into existence, nor the foundation for their success; they were read for entertainment, but entertainment presented under the banner of public good. As a result, their eidolons had to be figures of trust and of some social standing, not an anonymous club of experts nor your friend living in London.

Their printers also happily supplied their fans with multiple formats of collected editions of the once ephemeral *Tatler* and *Spectator* papers, with an appealing range in prices and formats. The *Tatler* advertised the price per volume for legitimate duodecimo as 2*s* 6*d.,* printed on "good paper" with "new Elzevir Letter" (a small, elegant Dutch type face associated with finely printed small format books), while collectors could choose between paying 10*s* 6*p* for the octavo volume on "medium paper," versus 21*s* for "royal paper." Buyers could feel confident that they were purchasing the genuine edition because of the style and format of its "running title," which is reproduced in the advertisement. Jacob Tonson published the first collected editions of the *Spectator* by subscription in January 1712. Tonson demonstrated his confidence in his merchandizing of the *Spectator*, offering it in both octavo and duodecimo format, the latter advertised as "a neat pocket edition" in the 18 January issue.[157]

As one critic has admiringly noted, in Tonson's hands "the *Spectator* was one of the greatest publishing sensations of the eighteenth century."[158] Tonson subsequently published fifteen matching volumes of the complete *Tatler*, *Spectator*, and *Guardian*. If this was not enough to fill the fan's bookcase, by 1737 one could purchase *The Mottoes of the Spectators, Tatlers, and Guardians,*

[155] *Tatler*, III: 363. By 1709, Steele had not only had successful comedies staged, married and buried an heiress, edited the *London Gazette*, and joined the Whig Kit-Kat Club, but he had also fathered an illegitimate child with the niece of the publisher Jacob Tonson, nearly killed a man in a London duel, was frequently attacked in the press by name by Tory commentators, and was constantly being harassed by creditors.

[156] *Spectator*, I: 44. [157] Bond, "The Text of the Spectator," p. 111.

[158] Wilkinson, "The Complete *Spectator*: A Bibliographical History," Abstract.

*Translated into English* and there was also *A General Index to the Spectators, Tatlers, and Guardians* to round out one's collection. With Jacob (the younger) and Richard Tonson's 1753 edition, one could purchase a set complete with illustrations designed by the popular artist and illustrator Frances Hayman, keyed to the essays by number. The unadorned ephemeral sheet has been transformed into an enduring literary collectible.

## 4.1 Spinoffs, Rivals, and Duds

The *Tatler* emboldened a flock of imitators shortly after its initial publication, but none of which gained the traction enjoyed by the initial paper. While some used the name to make the connection – the *Tatling Harlot* (3 issues in August 1709), *Titt for Tatt* (5 issues in 1710), and the *Tory Tatler* (16 issues, November 1710–December 1711) – others spun off the "family tree" of Isaac Bickerstaff, such the *Gazette A-la-Mode: or Tom Brown's Ghost* (5 issues, May–June 1709), narrated by Sir Thomas Whipstaff.[159] The *Female Tatler* (1709–1710) discussed previously openly attached itself to the successful *Tatler* in its first issue in its first line: "I Hope *Isaac Bickerstaff*, Esp; will not think I invade his Property, by undertaking a Paper of this kind, since *Tatling* was ever adjudg'd peculiar to our Sex," states Mrs. Crackenthorpe, and she insists that "my Design is not to Rival his Performance, or in the least prejudice the Reputation he has so deservedly gain'd."[160]

The *Female Tatler,* which as we have seen previously engaged in a vigorous contest with the *British Apollo* for readers, came into being on July 8, 1709, only two issues after "Mrs. Jenny Distaff," Bickerstaff's half-sister has taken over writing the *Tatler* while her brother is in the country on business in issue #36 July 2, 1709. The character of Jenny Distaff, believed by some to have been written by Addison, only contributed five issues, #10, 33, 36, 37, and 38; one cannot help but think that the addition of a female eidolon in this already popular series must have provided some encouragement to the writer of the *Female Tatler.*[161] This is particularly true as Jenny Distaff makes it clear that she is a woman writing about things that interest women. In her first paper, May 3, 1709, Jenny Distaff explains that she has been entrusted by her brother with "all the Papers in his Closet, which he has left open for my Use on this Occasion" (I: 87). She discusses some of the books she finds there, including *The Batchelor's Scheme for Governing his Wife* ("I have not Patience with these unreasonable Expectations") and the sixth part in Tonson's *Poetical*

[159] Osell, "Tatling Women in the Public Sphere," p. 285; see McLeod, *Graphical Directory* for the publication runs of the imitators.

[160] The *Female Tatler*, #1, Friday July 8, 1709.

[161] *Tatler*, I: 261.

*Miscellanies*, which itself had been published the day before the paper was issued. This volume with its "Collection of the best Pastorals that have hitherto appear'd in England," pleases her more, especially since the best in her opinion was by a woman, "where all our little Weaknesses are laid open in a Manner more just, and with truer Raillery, than ever Man yet hit upon," Anne Finch, Countess of Winchelsea's "A Pastoral Dialogue between Two Shepherdesses" (I: 89–90). Jenny Distaff continued her focus on matters pertaining to women and relations between the sexes, declaring in #36 that "you must expect the Advices you meet with in this Paper to be such, as more immediately and naturally fall under the Consideration of our Sex" namely "Love in all its Forms" (I: 261).

Likewise, the *Female Tatler*, as we saw in the previous section, used a decidedly feminine persona to encourage readers of both sexes to find its contexts amusing and instructive without restricting itself to matters of the heart. Rather than reporting from various coffee houses, Mrs. Crackenthorpe dates her entries as being from "my Own Apartment," where she hosts twice weekly "a very great Assembly of both Sexes"; guests range in social status from "his Grace my Lord Duke, to Mr. *Sagathei* the Spruce Mercer" and their wives attend. Her intent, much like that stated in the *Review* and then the *Tatler*, is to "gently to correct Vices and Vanities which some of Distinction, as well as others, willfully commit," without reflecting on any individual, thus promoting "Religion, Virtue, and Sobriety." She concludes by defending herself from those that say, "I write this Paper meerly for the Profit that may accrue to me by it." Following Steele's pattern, the opening numbers of the paper are to be distributed for free; in order to avoid any confusion, the *Female Tatler* was only published on Monday, Wednesday, and Fridays, the days when the *Tatler* does not appear.

Rather than claiming kinship to Mr. Bickerstaff, Mrs. Crackenthorpe instead is told by Lady Coupler "she could not propose any Match half so suitable as Mr. Bickerstaff and my self" and that their offspring would all be "Bishops, Judges and Recorders, and the Daughters Behns, Philips's and Daciers," a fascinating combination of abstract male authority figures and actual women writers.[162] Mrs. Crackenthorpe hastily declines the offer by Lady Coupler to introduce this idea to Mr. Bickerstaff but does say she'd welcome an acquaintance with his sister Jenny Distaff and that Lady Coupler could invite him to attend her public day assembly. References to the *Tatler* and Bickerstaff are frequent but typically in a joking complementary style; as Iona Italia has noted,

[162] The *Female Tatler*, #2, Friday July 8, 1709.

the periodical presents itself as a "female answer to Steele's publication and continually defines itself in reference to the *Tatler*."[163]

The case is very different between the two rival versions of the *Female Tatler*, which, as we saw in the controversy with the *British Apollo*, seems focused on conflicts over social status. It is a case of dueling personas, as Powell observes, "both eidolons try to persuade the reader that the rival paper is connected to a lower-class male, and so her work is the one the astute reader ought to choose."[164] After issue #51, Mrs. Crackenthorpe, however, bows out, claiming "resenting the Affront offer'd to her by some rude Citizens, altogether unacquainted with her Person," turning the editorship over to a "Society of Modest Ladies, who in their turns will oblige the Publick with whatever they shall meet with, that will be Diverting, Innocent, or Instructive."[165] This "Society of Ladies," consists of Lucinda, Emilia, Arabella, Rosella, Artesia, and Sophronia, recalling those earlier clubs whose members are named but unlike them not creating a strong sense of individual personality.

Although the *Female Tatler* made use of a great many letters, many, if not all, are fictitious. Likewise, there are advertisements which are clearly jokes or spoofs. There is internal evidence that the invitations to readers to participate are also fictious. Unlike other sociable periodicals we have explored, the practical details of how and where readers are to submit letters is not a regular feature. On the one hand, at the start of issue #68, Mrs. Baldwin, the publisher, states "I have read till my Eyes ake; and confess that looking on this help of Letters before me, I have no reason to Complain for want of Intelligence from Abroad." Likewise, in Issue #53 above the advertisements, there is an announcement that "A Table of Fame for the Ladies well be Publish'd as soon as Materials can be Collected, to which end, the Publick are desired to Contribute, and it will be gratefully acknowledg'd." But in fact, in neither instance is any information given about where or how to send such correspondence. Iona Italia suggests that the invitation to readers to send materials to the *Female Tatler* is genuine, citing #7 where Mrs. Crackenthorpe wishes that only "Gentlemen or Ladies please to write any thing . . . it will be kindly receiv'd." However, as Italia also points out, this is followed by Mrs. Crackenthorpe's suggestion that those interested in corresponding should first attend her public days, events which are clearly fictional.[166]

Why did this lively and contested periodical sink into the footnotes of literary history rather than rise into the canon? As we have seen, with both the *Tatler* and the *Spectator*, the identities behind the eidolons of Isaac Bickerstaff and

[163] Italia, *Rise of Literary Journalism*, p. 64. [164] Powell, *Performing Authorship*, p. 70.
[165] The *Female Tatler*, #51, Monday October 31, 1709.
[166] The *Female Tatler*, #7, July 22, 1709.

Mr. Spectator were an immediate source of conversation among contemporary readers and Steele and Addison appear to have become quickly associated with them. In contrast, the authorship of the *Female Tatler* has continued to be debated well through the twentieth century and twenty-first centuries. Some, like the writers of the *British Apollo*, still ascribe the first version it to the dramatist Thomas Baker, while others subsequently detect the styles of Delarivier Manley, Bernard Mandeville, Eliza Haywood, and possibly Susanna Centlivre. As Paul Anderson observed "such a variety of pseudonyms is bewildering to the reader who would like to discover the real person or persons concerned in writing *The Female Tatler.*"[167]

Even though it ran for 115 issues, there was no collected, bound edition for the *Female Tatler.* There is also no indication in its contents that its publishers, either Benjamin Bragge or Anne Baldwin, made any attempt to market it as a collectible publication or offered readers copies of single sheets of any missed issues or ways of compiling them that we find characterizing other only moderately successful homages to the *Tatler* and *Spectator*, such as Charles Povey's, *The Visions of Sir Heister Ryley* (1711) or Sir Richard Blackmore's *The Lay Monk*, published in a single-volume collection as *The Lay-Monastry* (1714).

The *Female Tatler* is a good example of a periodical that embraced many of the features of popular papers which preceded it and was more immediately successful than most of its rivals. Nevertheless, it failed to make the leap from popular ephemera to collectible literary commodity. Compared to the *Tatler* and the *Spectator*, its was a fleeting fame. It does not appear that the *Female Tatler* sold copies because of the identity of its author(s); it did not create a participatory audience through interacting with correspondence. It lacked the community-building appeal of central, celebrity eidolon, much less did it possess elegant prose, to help propel it into the canon of English literature. Instead, its publishers, unlike Jacob Tonson, moved on to other short-lived ventures.

## 5 Epilogue: From Sociable Clubs to the Voice of Authority, 1740–1750s: Eliza Haywood's the *Female Spectator* and Samuel Johnson's the *Rambler*

> ... Building topical authority is one of the best ways to rank higher in Google's search results ... one thing Google says over and over again is your content should demonstrate your authority and expertise in the topic.
>
> –Eb Gargano, 2023

[167] Anderson, "Splendor out of Scandal," p. 286.

> . . . Yes, there are other blogs out there about the same thing you want to write about. Question: So why is your blog different? Answer: Because of *you. You* are what makes *your* blog different. It's about *your* perspective, *your* creativity, the value *you* add.
>
> –Joshua Fields Millburn and Ryan Nicodemus[168]

Two successful publications in the mid- and late-eighteenth century, Eliza Haywood's the *Female Spectator* and Samuel Johnson's the *Rambler*, while clearly building on the audience for periodicals created by the earlier sociable journals that had been based on an active reader participation, were in several respects different from their forerunners. What changed from those earlier social periodicals such as the *Athenian Mercury* and the *Tatler* which enthusiastically solicited their readers' contributions, to the *Female Spectator* and the *Rambler*? What did they offer their readers rather than the sense of belonging to a social club of like-minded people, sharing their literary creations and determining content?

Once again, we find a continuation of those by now well-established conventions, an eidolon standing in for a named author, the use of the letter format to frame content, and the presence of a "club" representing multiple social points of view. With Haywood and Johnson's periodicals, however, there are significant differences in that content and also the relationship between the readers and the authors. Both of these periodicals, I would argue, achieved their success by inhabiting the form of the earlier journals, the eidolon and letter format, while rejecting its dynamic, the participatory culture, and reliance on amateur reader-authors for content.

Although authorship of the *Female Spectator* (1744–1746) remains contested, many of Eliza Haywood's contemporaries as well as recent critics attribute the majority of the work to her. There has never been any confusion of the authorship of the *Rambler* (1750–1752); while Samuel Johnson was completing the monumental task of assembling and writing the *English Dictionary*, his indefatigable chroniclers James Boswell and Hester Thrale tell us that he turned to essay writing as a source of immediate income. When viewed through the lens of earlier periodicals as platforms for social media and participatory culture, we see in these two titles a shift, which is reflected in their format and marketing, as well as how the writers seem to have viewed their readers as contributors.

There are many familiar features in the *Female Spectator* that contributed to the success of its forerunners. As with the *Spectator*, there is a "club" to assist the narrator, each of whom embodies a different stage in female life and point of

[168] Gargano, "How to Use Topical Authority to Boost Your Ranking and Grow Your Blog Traffic"; Milburn and Nicedemus, "How to Start a Successful Blog in 2023."

view. Like the issues of the *Tatler* using the eidolon of Bickerstaff's sister, the subject is typically matters of the heart–marriage and female virtue. This narrator, however, seems determined to hold the readers at arm's length. As she states in the first issue, the eidolon of the *Female Spectator* bases her essays on her own experiences, augmented by essays contributed by the other ladies of the club, and "any others I may hereafter correspond with," not letters left at a coffee house directed to her by unknown persons. In sharp contrast to earlier periodical authors and their clubs, who provide a platform for their readers' contributions, she notes that her readers, "provided the Entertainment be agreeable, will not be interested from which Quarter it comes": all the content will appear "under the general Title of *The Female Spectator*, and how many Contributors soever there may happen to be to the Work, they are to be consider'd only as several Members of one Body, of which I am the Mouth."[169] The readers' friendly community of correspondents also has been replaced by "spies," who have been planted not only in all the London social gathering spots, in Bath and Tunbridge, but also abroad as well as abroad, measures which negate the need for readers to supply any content whatsoever. Rejecting the pattern found in the *Tatler* and *Spectator,* the narrator notes that if there are gaps in content, she will turn to "the Ancients" for her examples to avoid the possibility of scandal from readers attempting to uncover contemporary references.

Readers of Haywood's risqué early fiction *Fantomina* may be surprised by this Female Spectator's denunciation of giddy young women intent on experiencing life to the fullest. Instead of reading romances and visiting the theatre, the readers of the *Female Spectator* were encouraged to study philosophy, along with history and geography. "It is very much, by the Choice we make of Subjects for our Entertainment," the narrator observes in the first issue, "that the refined Taste distinguishes itself from the vulgar and more gross."[170] The contents of the essays cover a variety of topics and have led recently to considerable critical discussion as to their exact nature: with its stress on education and moral improvement, does Haywood in her stories offer her female readers a means of subverting social limitations or of surviving within them?[171] Most telling, Eve Tavor Bannet has pointed to the ways in which the *Female Spectator* directly challenges the ways in which the *Spectator* purports to educate and elevate its female readers; the Female Spectator makes clear from the beginning her "Power to be in some measure both useful and entertaining to the Publick," and her intention "to be as universally read as

[169] Haywood, *The Female Spectator*, I: 5. [170] Haywood, *The Female Spectator*, I: 1.

[171] See the collection edited by Wright and Newman *Fair Philosopher: Eliza Haywood and the Female Spectator* for a good overview of the debates.

possible."[172] Within the range of characters and problems introduced through the fictious letters, mostly by Haywood, however, Richardo Miguel-Alfonso has argued that the narrator stands in an elevated position of moral authority based on her experiences: "the difference between Haywood and her readers is clear from the beginning," he suggests, with the Female Spectator established not a friend but the "counselor" for her "inexperienced readers," producing a tone not unlike Defoe's Scandalous Club, who, as we have seen, announced that his "we" was indeed "I."[173]

As Kathryn King observes, by the time of the *Female Spectator* is published "Haywood is no longer the 'bedraggled' Grub Street hack churning out copy for her bookseller," but instead a literary professional, heavily involved in the print trade, "an editor and chief writer whose job would have included obtaining contributions from other writers and coordinating production."[174] The contents have shifted from the miscellany format, pointedly eschewing "news," and resisting ephemerality both in content and packaging. Unlike Motteux pleading for reader contributions to keep the *Gentleman's Journal* going, the fate of the *Female Spectator*'s does not appear to have rested on its receiving content from unpaid readers. The reader is offered a single topic essay each month, not a compendium of unrelated questions and miscellaneous verse. When we look at this periodical through the lens of social media and participation culture, the *Female Spectator* is much less concerned with soliciting readers' questions or contributions than serving as vehicle for an authoritative moral voice, that of the Female Spectator/ Haywood.

In addition, as opposed to sociable periodicals such as the *Athenian Mercury* and the original *Spectator* with their multiple appearances throughout the week, the *Female Spectator* was printed and published by Thomas Gardner in monthly installments. The initial form is no longer a double-columned ephemeral broadsheet or pamphlet publication; typically, the *Female Spectator* offered readers a substantial sixty-four octavo pages, which subsequently were, like its predecessors, gathered in individual "books" (Figure 10). As Patrick Spedding has documented, each individual collected book from the two-year run enjoyed two editions and there were nine editions of the complete set published in four elegant volumes.[175] The popularity of the *Female Spectator* rested not on its ephemeral format nor on its interaction with loyal readers who created content; instead, readers are offered a charmingly packaged collectible item, done

[172] Bannet, "Haywood's Spectator and the Female World," p. 46.
[173] Miguel-Alfonso, "Social Conservatism," pp. 34–5.
[174] King, *A Political Biography of Eliza Haywood*, p. 116.
[175] Spedding, *Bibliography*, p. 432.

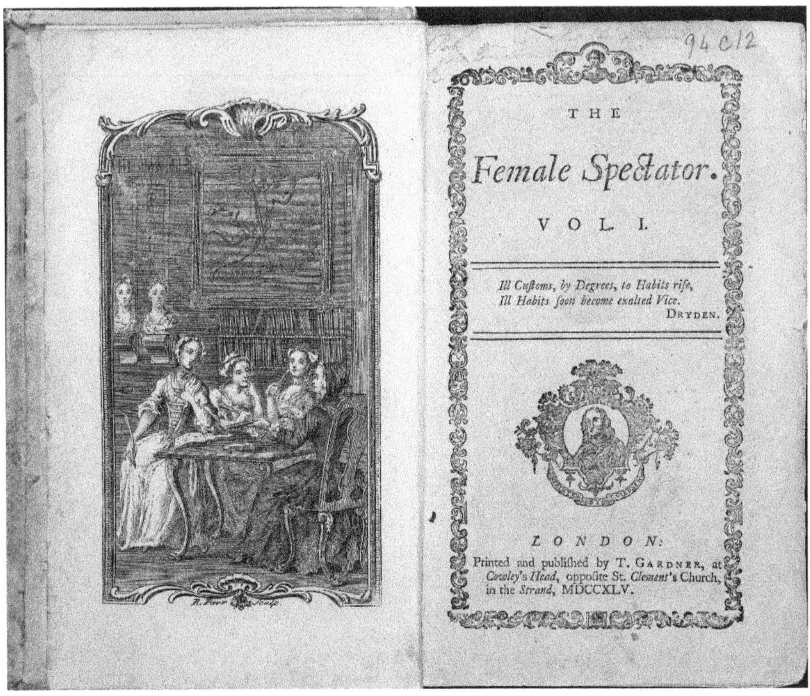

THE

Female Spectator.

VOL. I.

Ill Customs, by Degrees, to Habits rise,
Ill Habits soon become exalted Vice.
DRYDEN.

LONDON:
Printed and published by T. GARDNER, at Cowley's Head, opposite St. Clement's Church, in the Strand, MDCCXLV.

**Figure 10.** *The Female Spectator* (1746). (c) The British Library Board. 94.c.12.

through corporate authorship, under the guidance of an experienced professional writer, Eliza Haywood.

Like the *Female Spectator*, as Johnson's biographers and critics have commented, the *Rambler* in its original periodical format was not an immediate success (Figure 11). In part this might be attributed to Johnson's openly ambivalent attitude towards many of the conventions that had made earlier periodicals popular. While very much aware of the conventions of the genre, there is evidence that Johnson apparently deliberately rejected them. W. J. Bate observes that in writing the *Rambler*, Johnson was "on his guard against the usual – and expected – topicality of the periodical essay: "I have never complied with temporary curiosity, nor enabled my readers to discuss the topick of the day," Johnson declares.[176] Likewise, initially he was determined to keep his authorship secret, apparently in hopes of avoiding having to have the expected interactions with his readers and responding to their letters. Even though he did use epistles, supposedly from readers, to frame the content of some essays, in spite of occasionally including directions where letters might be

[176] *The Rambler*, 3: xxvi

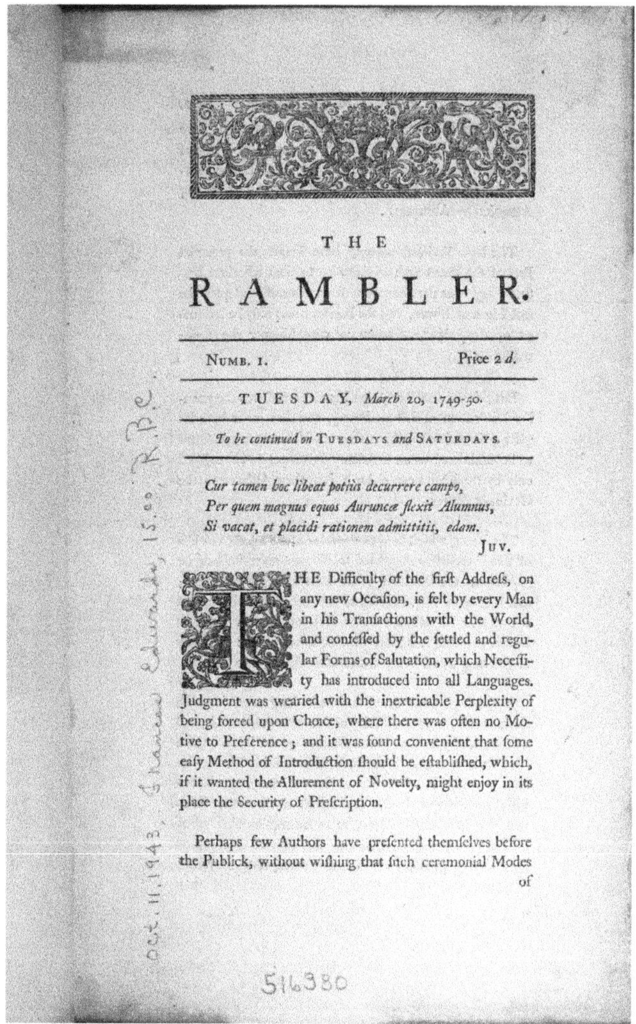

THE

RAMBLER.

NUMB. I. Price 2 *d.*

TUESDAY, *March* 20, 1749-50.

*To be continued on* TUESDAYS *and* SATURDAYS.

*Cur tamen hoc libeat potiùs decurrere campo,*
*Per quem magnus equos Auruncæ flexit Alumnus,*
*Si vacat, et placidi rationem admittitis, edam.*
JUV.

THE Difficulty of the firſt Addreſs, on any new Occaſion, is felt by every Man in his Tranſactions with the World, and confeſſed by the ſettled and regular Forms of Salutation, which Neceſſity has introduced into all Languages. Judgment was wearied with the inextricable Perplexity of being forced upon Choice, where there was often no Motive to Preference; and it was found convenient that ſome eaſy Method of Introduction ſhould be eſtabliſhed, which, if it wanted the Allurement of Novelty, might enjoy in its place the Security of Preſcription.

Perhaps few Authors have preſented themſelves before the Publick, without wiſhing that ſuch ceremonial Modes of

**Figure 11.** *The Rambler*, no. 1 (1752). By permission of Harry Ransom Center, University of Texas, Austin.

sent, Johnson apparently told Samuel Richardson that "he had never intended to use random letters from outside correspondents," which caused some hard feelings in readers who sent letters that were ignored.[177] While sixty-five of the two hundred and eight *Ramblers* do use epistles to structure the essay, as Manushag Powell observed, they are "(almost) all written by Johnson," resulting in "a large body of letters written apparently from various persons to Mr. Rambler, but in fact to himself from himself for the benefit of strangers."[178]

[177] *The Rambler*, 3: 367, fnt 4. [178] Powell, "Johnson and His 'Readers,'" p. 573.

Instead of interacting with the questions and challenges of his readers, Johnson is not writing the periodical essay as it was popular at the time, but instead offering readers a "direct moral essay."[179] Johnson states in his final issue #208 that he had deliberately avoided many of the expected features of a periodical:

> I have never complied with temporary curiosity, nor enabled my readers to discuss the topick of the day; I have rarely exemplified my assertions by living characters; in my papers, no man could look for censures of his enemies, or praises of himself; and they only were expected to peruse them, whose passions left them leisure for abstracted truth, and whom virtue could please by its naked dignity.[180]

Unlike the contents of its predecessors, mingling information with deft social commentary mixed with scandal, and with a seemingly accessible relationship between writer and reader, the contents of the *Rambler* are the iteration of Samuel Johnson's views, illustrations of his philosophy only. Indeed, the reader is not really interested in or concerned with "Mr. Rambler," but instead with Dr. Johnson: As Helen Deutsch has observed Johnson inspired in his time and since a phenomenon she calls "author love," the desire "to know the author himself," both the public quotable persona and the private man revealed in personal anecdotes.[181] "To write an interpretative introduction to the *Rambler* is to write a general and interpretative introduction to Johnson," observes Bate, "here, more than anywhere else, we have the essence of Johnson."[182] While the individual issues never enjoyed more than 500 copies in a run, like the *Female Spectator*, the success of this periodical came when it was reprinted in bound, book form: it appeared in a folio edition in 1750–1752 as well as a duodecimo edition (1752), and had gone through nine editions by 1779.

The *Female Spectator* and the *Rambler* offer readers a very different experience from the earliest sociable periodicals. As the contents moved from the miscellany format of news, verse, and queries, there was a shift from the participatory, social culture of the periodicals of the 1690s and early 1700s where anonymous clubs would provide answers to the questions of subscribers; there seems to have been another shift with the emphasis on the celebrity eidolon and contents in which readers might participate and decode topical references. Although preserving many of the conventional features that

[179] *The Rambler*, 3: xxx. [180] *The Rambler*, 5: 316.

[181] Deutsch, *Loving Dr. Johnson*, p. 4. Here I am diverging somewhat from Manushag Powell's use of this term to explain the dual nature public-private of the eidolon (*Performing Authorship*, p. 26) to suggest that "Dr. Johnson" was at this point a social construction, who did not need or desire a fictional persona to narrate his views.

[182] *The Rambler*, 3: ix.

characterized earlier periodical writing, by the mid-century, the eidolon is an authoritative moral voice speaking on universal human problems. The shared experiences of writers inviting readers to become authors, of readers interacting sociably with a celebrity eidolon has been replaced by this admirable authoritative voice. While all of the early periodicals claimed to be written with the intent in Haywood's words to reform "the Faulty, and give an innocent amusement to those who are not so," the experience of the reader by the middle of the century is not to provide poetry, queries, or information, but to ponder with gratitude the illuminating representation of human nature. The imagined social relationship between reader and writer found in participatory social media has been transformed into that of an appreciative but silent audience. Johnson in the last issue of the *Rambler* seems to note with relief that since "my principal design [has been] to inculcate wisdom or piety," he has been released from gratifying correspondents' desires for appearing in print.[183] By the time of the *Female Spectator* and the *Rambler*, the periodical form's early function as a platform for participatory literary culture has become an enabling fiction and the eidolon a voice of moral authority for the reader to admire – what results is the emphasis on the literary essay as we conceive of it today, and, clearly, is the forerunner to a successful blog on Substack, the writer speaking directly to the subscriber in a voice at once personal, attractive, and authoritative.

******

Of course, not all periodicals in the latter part of the eighteenth century eschewed accepting content from unpaid readers, the *Ladies Magazine; or Entertaining Companion for the Fair Sex, Appropriated Solely to Their Use and Amusement* (1770–1847) being a notable example. Edward Cave's *Gentleman's Magazine* had been the first to use the French term "magazine" to distinguish its contents, being a "storehouse" of miscellaneous content. As Jennie Batchelor has noted, this shift in the nomenclature from periodical to magazine may seem minor, but magazines are defined by "their miscellaneous character and the absence of the kind of unifying perspective provided by eidolons such as Mr. Spectator, the Female Spectator, or the Old Maid."[184] After the 1810s and 1820s, the *Ladies Magazine* also began to shift from a "culture of nonpayment" to a more complex commercial one.[185] Magazines, one might argue, preserved elements of participatory culture after the periodical became defined as its essay.

The model of participatory culture as we discuss it now in a digital environment was a viable and familiar literary ecology for periodical readers in the

[183] *The Rambler*, 5: 319, 317. [184] Batchelor, *The Ladies Magazine*, p. 15

[185] Batchelor, *The Ladies Magazine*, p. 129–31.

latter part of the seventeenth century and beginning of the eighteenth century. The initially ephemeral pamphlet and broadsheet publications utilized the latest communication technology, the Penny Post, to create its audience and content makers. As Henry Jenkins has observed of the emergence of digital technology, it "did not make fandom more participatory, but . . . [it] did dramatically expand who got to participate."[186] In studying it, we have traditionally concentrated on one small element, the essay, and thus we have lost sight of the complex, dynamic literary culture that originally created and sustained it. Focusing on changes and choices created today by digital forms and social media as unprecedented, we likewise lose a sense of our own connections with the past, of how we, too, are part of that larger story of how literary cultures embrace changing technologies.

---

[186] Jenkins, *Participatory Culture*, p. 17.

# Bibliography

Anderson, Paul Bunyan. "The History and Authorship of Mrs. Crackenthorpe's Female Tatler." *Modern Philology* 28, no.3 (1931): 354–50.

Anderson, Paul Buyan. "Splendor out of Scandal: The Lucinda-Artesia Papers in the Female Tatler." *Philological Quarterly* 15 (1936): 286–300.

*Athenian Mercury*. London: John Dunton, 1690–97.

Austen, Jane. *Northanger Abbey, Lady Susan, the Watsons, Sanditon*. Edited by Claudia L. Johnson, John Davie, and James Kinsley. Oxford: Oxford University Press, 2008. https://doi.org/10.1093/owc/9780199535545.001.0001.

Backscheider, Paula R. *Elizabeth Singer Rowe and the Development of the English Novel*. Baltimore, MD: Johns Hopkins University Press, 2013.

Ballatore, A., and S. Natale. "E-readers and the Death of the Book: Or, New Media and the Myth of the Disappearing Medium." *New Media & Society* 18 (2016): 2379–94. https://doi.org/10.1177/1461444815586984.

Bannet, Eve Tavor. "Epistolary Commerce." In *The Spectator: Emerging Discourses*. Edited by Donald J. Newman, 220–47. Newark, NJ: University of Delaware Press, 2005.

Bannet, Eve Tavor. "Haywood's Spectator and the Female World." In *Fair Philosopher: Eliza Haywood and the Female Spectator*. Edited by Lynn Marie Wright, and Donald J. Newman, 41–62. Lewisburg, PA: Bucknell University Press, 2006.

Batchelor, Jennie. *The Lady's Magazine (1770–1832) and the Making of Literary History*. Edinburgh: Edinburgh University Press, 2022.

Batchelor, Jennie, and Manushag N. Powell, eds. *Women's Periodicals and Print Culture in Britain, 1690–1820s the Long Eighteenth Century*. Edinburgh: Edinburgh University Press, 2018.

Bateson, F. W. "The Errata in the Tatler." *Review of English Studies* 5 (1929): 155–66.

Belcher, William F. "The Sale and Distribution of the British Apollo." In *Studies in the Early English Periodical*. Edited by Richmond P. Bond, 73–102. Chapel Hill, NC: University of North Carolina Press, 1957.

Benedict, Barbara M. "Publishing and Reading Poetry." In *The Cambridge Companion to Eighteenth-Century Poetry*. Edited by John Sitter, 63–82. Cambridge: Cambridge University Press, 2001.

Berry, Helen. "Dunton, John (1659–1732), bookseller." *Oxford Dictionary of National Biography*. September 23, 2004; Accessed October 6, 2022.

Berry, Helen. *Gender, Society, and Print Culture in Late Stuart England: The Cultural World of the Athenian Mercury*. Aldershott: Ashgate, 2003.

Blackmore, Richard. *The [Lay]-Monastery; Consisting of Essays, Discourse, &c; Published Singly under the Title of the [Lay]-[Monk]; Being the Sequel of the Spectators*. 2nd ed. London: Anne Baldwin, 1713.

Bolter, Jay David. *The Digital Plenitude: The Decline of Elite Culture and the Rise of New Media*. Boston, MA: MIT Press, 2019.

Bond, Donald F. "The First Printing of the *Spectator*." *Modern Philology* 47, no.3 (1950): 164–77.

Bond, Donald F. "The Text of the 'Spectator.'" *Studies in Bibliography* 5 (1952/1953): 109–28.

Bond, Richmond P. ed. *New Letters to the Tatler and Spectator*. Austin, TX: University of Texas Press, 1959.

Bond, Richmond P. *The Tatler: The Making of a Literary Journal*. Cambridge, MA: Harvard University Press, 1971.

Botein, Stephen, Jack R. Censer, and Harriet Ritvo. "The Periodical Press in Eighteenth-Century English and French Society: A Cross Cultural Approach." *Comparative Studies in Society and History* 23, no.3 (1981): 464–90.

Bowers, Terence. "Universalizing Sociability: The Spectator, Civic Enfranchisement, and the Rule(s) of the Public Sphere." In *The Spectator: Emerging Discourses*. Edited by Donald J. Newman, 150–74. Newark, NJ: University of Delaware Press, 2005.

*British Apollo*. London: John Mayo, 1708–11.

Briscoe, Samuel. *Familiar Letters of Love, Gallantry, and Several Other Occasions*. London: Samuel Briscoe, 1718–1724.

*British Newspapers and Periodicals 1641–1700: A Short Title Catalogue of Serials Printed in England, Scotland, Ireland, and British America*. Compiled by Carolyn Nelson and Matthew Seccombe. New York, NY: The Modern Languages Association, 1987.

*British Royal Proclamations Relating to America 1603–1783*. Edited by Clarence S. Brigham. New York, NJ: Burt Franklin, 1968; reprint 1911 edition American Antiquarian Society.

*Broadview Anthology of British Literature: The Restoration and the Eighteenth Century*, 2nd ed. Edited by Joseph Black, Leonard Conolly, Kate Flint, et al. Peterborough: Broadview Press, 2012.

Brumell, George. *The Local Posts of London, 1680–1840*. Bournemouth: n.p., 1938.

Carnell, Rachel. "Slipping from Secret History to Novel." *Eighteenth-Century Fictions* 28, no.1 (2015): 1–24.

Clery, E. J. *The Feminization Debate: Literature, Commerce and Luxury*. London: Palgrave Macmillan, 2004. https://doi.org/10.1057/9780230509047_3.

Cook, David. "Swift after Cowley." *Restoration* 44, no.2 (2020): 37–54.

Coperías-Aguilar, María José. "Between Fictionality and Reality: The 'Novels' in the *Gentleman's Journal*." *Sederi* 32 (2022): 9–29.

Cowan, Brian. "Daniel Defoe's Review and the Transformations of the English Periodical." *The Huntington Library Quarterly* 77, no.1 (2014): 79–110.

Cowan, Brian. "Mr. Spectator and the Coffeehouse Public Sphere." *Eighteenth-Century Studies* 37, no.3 (2004): 345–66. www.jstor.org/stable/25098064.

Cunningham, Robert Newton. *Peter Anthony Motteux, 1663–1718: A Biographical and Critical Study*. Oxford: Basil Blackwell, 1933.

Davies, Godfrey. "English Political Sermons, 1603–1640." *Huntington Library Quarterly* 3, no.1 (1939):1–22.

Defoe, Daniel. *Review*. 9 Vols, 2 parts. Edited by John McVeagh, London: Pickering and Chatto, 2011.

DeMers, Jayson. "The 7 Biggest Secrets of Social Media Influencers." *X Business*. https://business.twitter.com/en/blog/secrets-of-social-media-influencers.html.

Deutsch, Helen. *Loving Dr. Johnson*. Chicago, IL: University of Chicago, 2005.

Downie, J. A. "Reflections on the Origins of the Periodical Essay: A Review Article.," *Prose Studies* 12, no.3 (1989): 296–302. https://doi.org/10.1080/01440358908586381.

Downie, J. A "Stating Facts Right about Defoe's Review." In *Telling People What to Think: Early Eighteenth-Century Periodicals from the Review to the Rambler*. Edited by. J. A. Downie and Thomas N. Corns, 8–22. London: Frank Cass, 1993.

Dunton, John. *The Life and Errors of John Dunton, Citizen of London*. 2 Vols. (1818). Ed. John Nichols. Cambridge: Cambridge University Press, 2014.

Dykstal, Timothy. "The Politics of Taste in the 'Spectator.'" *The Eighteenth Century* 35, no.1 (1994): 46–63.

Eagleton, Terry. *The Function of Criticism: From the Spectator to Post-Structuralism*. London: Verso, 1984.

Ezell, Margaret J. M. "The Gentleman's Journal and the Commercialization of Restoration Coterie Literary Practices." *Modern Philology* 89, no.3 (1992): 323–40.

Ezell, Margaret J. M. "Late Seventeenth-Century Women Writers and the Penny Post: Early Social Media Forms and Access to Celebrity." In *Material Cultures of Early Modern Women's Writing*. Edited by Patricia J. Pender and Rosalind Smith, 140–58. London: Palgrave Macmillan, 2014.

Ezell, Margaret J. M. "Learning the News: Pamphlet Mercuries and Newsbooks." In *The Oxford English Literary History: Volume V: 1645–1714: The Later Seventeenth Century: Companion Volume*. Oxford: Oxford University Press, 2017. https://doi.org/10.1093/oso/9780191849572.001.0001.

Ezell, Margaret J. M. "Mr. Spectator on Readers and the Conspicuous Consumption of Literature." *Literature Compass* 1, no.1 (2004). https://doi.org/10.1111/j.1741-4113.2004.00014.x.

Ezell, Margaret J. M. *Social Authorship and the Advent of Print*. Baltimore, MD: The Johns Hopkins University Press, 1999.

Flynn, Christopher. "Defoe's Review: Textual Editing and New Media." *Digital Defoe* 1, no.1 (2009):18–20. https://english.illinoisstate.edu/digitaldefoe/archive/spring09/multimedia/index.shtml. ISSN 1948–1802 (online).

Foster, Dorothy. "The Earliest Precursor of Our Present-Day Monthly Miscellanies." *PMLA* 32, no.1 (1917): 22–58.

Gargano, Eb. "How to Use Topical Authority to Boost Your Rankings and Grow Your Blog Traffic." *Productiveblogging.com*. www.productiveblogging.com/topical-authority/.

Gay, John. *The Present State of Wit*. London: 1711.

*Gentleman's Journal*. London: Robert Baldwin, 1692–1694.

Gerrard, Christine. "Hill, Aaron (1685–1750), Writer and Entrepreneur." *Oxford Dictionary of National Biography*. September 23, 2004; Accessed June 26, 2023.

Gomez, Jeff. *Print is Dead: Books in Our Digital Age*. New York, NY: Palgrave Macmillan, 2007.

Graham, Walter. "Thomas Aker, Mrs. Manley, and the *Female Tatler*." *Modern Philology* 34, no.3 (1937): 267–72.

Graham, Walter. *English Literary Periodicals*. New York, NY: Thomas Nelson, 1930.

Haslett, Moyra. "Swift and Conversational Culture." *Eighteenth-Century Ireland/ Iris an dá chultúr* 29 (2014): 11–30.

Haywood, Eliza. *The Female Spectator*. 4 Volumes. London: Thomas Gardner, 1744.

Hobbs, Mary. *Early Seventeenth-Century Verse Miscellany Manuscripts*. Aldershot: Scolar Press, 1992.

"How to Build a Career as a Social Media Influencer." *The Economic Times*. https://economictimes.indiatimes.com/news/how-to/how-to-build-a-career-as-a-social-media-influencer/articleshow/95356598.cms?utm_source=contentofinterest&utm_medium=text&utm_campaign=cppst.

Italia, Iona. *The Rise of Literary Journalism in the Eighteenth Century: Anxious Employment*. London: Routledge, 2012.

Jack, Jane H. "The Periodical Essayists." In *From Dryden to Johnson: Volume 4: The Pelican Guides to English Literature*. Edited by Boris Ford, 182–194. Hammondsworth: Penguin, 1957.

Jenkins, Henry, Ravi Puroshotma, Katherine Clinton, Margaret Weigel, and Alice J. Robison. "Confronting the Challenges of Participatory Culture: Media Education for the 21st Century." 2005. www.newmedialiteracies.org/wp-content/uploads/pdfs/NMLWhitePaper.pdf . https://doi.org/10.7551/mitpress/8435.001.0001.

Jenkins, Henry, Sam Ford, and Joshua Green. *Spreadable Media: Creating Value and Meaning in a Networked Culture*. New York, NY: New York University Press, 2018.

Jenkins, Henry. *Fans, Bloggers, and Gamers: Exploring Participatory Culture*. New York, NY: New York University Press, 2006.

Johnson, Samuel. *The Rambler*. Volumes 3–5. *The Yale Edition of the Works of Samuel Johnson*. Edited by W. J. Bate and Albrecht B. Strauss. New Haven, CT: Yale University Press, 1969.

Justice, George. "The Spectator and Distance Education." In *The Spectator: Emerging Discourses*. Edited by Donald J. Newman, 265–300. Newark, NJ: University of Delaware Press, 2005.

King, Kathryn R. "Elizabeth Singer Rowe's Tactical Use of Print and Manuscript." In *Women's Writing and the Circulation of Ideas: Manuscript Publication England, 1550–1800*. Edited George L. Justice and Nathan Tinker, 158–81. Cambridge: Cambridge University Press, 2002.

King, Kathryn R. *A Political Biography of Eliza Haywood*. London: Routledge, 2012.

King, Rachael Scarborough. "All the News That's Fit to Print: The Eighteenth-Century Manuscript Newsletter." In *Travelling Chronicles: News and Newspapers from the Early Modern Period to the Eighteenth Century*. Edited by Siv Gøril Brandtzæg, Paul Goring, and Christine Watson, 95–118. Leiden: Brill, 2018. https://doi.org/10.1163/9789004362871_006.

King, Rachael Scarborough. "The Gazette, the Tatler, and the Making of the Periodical Essay: Form and Genre in Eighteenth-Century News." *The Papers of the Bibliographical Society of America* 114, no.1 (2020): 45–70.

Lauden, Heidi. "Birthing the Poet: Elizabeth Singer Rowe and the Athenian Mercury." *1650–1850: Ideas, Aesthetics, and Inquiries in the Early Modern Era* 22, no.2 (2015): 1–17.

Levy, Michelle, and Betty A. Schellenberg. *How and Why to Do Things with Eighteenth-Century Manuscripts*. Cambridge: Cambridge University Press, 2021.

Levy, Michelle. *Family Authorship and Romantic Print Culture*. Basingstoke: Palgrave, 2008.

Levy, Michelle. *Literary Manuscript Culture in Romantic Britain*. Edinburgh: Edinburgh University Press, 2020.

Lillie, Charles. *Original and Genuine Letters Sent to the Tatler and Spectator during the Time Those Works Were publishing. None of Which Have Been before Printed*. 2 Volumes. London: R. Harbin, 1725.

Logan, Lisa A. "'Dear Matron—': Constructions of Women in Eighteenth-Century American Periodical Advice Columns." *Studies in American Humor* 3, no.11 (2004): 57–63.

*London Gazette*. www.thegazette.co.uk/London.

Love, Harold. *Scribal Publication in Seventeenth-Century England*. Oxford: Clarendon Press, 1993.

Loveman, Kate. *Reading Fictions, 1660–1740: Deception in English Literary and Political Culture*. Burlington, VT: Ashgate, 2008.

Macaulay, Thomas Babington. *History of England from the Accession of James II*. 5 Vols. Philadelphia, PA: Porter & Coates, 1876.

Mackie, Erin. *Market a la Mode: Fashion, Commodity, and Gender in the Tatler and the Spectator*. Baltimore, MD: The Johns Hopkins University Press, 1997.

Marotti, Arthur. *Manuscript, Print, and the English Renaissance Lyric*. Ithaca, NY: Cornell University Press, 1995.

Marr, George S. *The Periodical Essayists of the Eighteenth Century*. London: James Clarke, 1923.

Marshall, Ashley. *Political Journalism in London, 1695–1720: Defoe, Swift, Steele and Their Contemporaries*. Woodbridge: Boydell and Brewer, 2020.

McBain, Jean. "'Love, Marriages, Mistresses, and the Like': Daniel Defoe's Scandal Club and an Emotional Community in Print." In *Passions, Sympathy and Print Culture: Public Opinion and Emotional Authenticity in Eighteenth-Century Britain*. Edited by. Heather Kerr and Robert Phiddian, 69–85. New York, NY: Palgrave Macmillan, 2016.

McCrea, Brian. *Addison and Steele Are Dead: The English Department, Its Canon, and the Professionalization of Literary Criticism*. Newark, NJ: University of Delaware Press, 1990.

McCrea. Brian. "The Virtue of Repetition: Mr. Spectator Trains Benjamin Franklin." In *The Spectator: Emerging Discourses*. Edited by Donald J. Newman, 248–64. Newark, NJ: University of Delaware Press, 2005.

McElligott, Jason, and Eve Patten. "The Perils of Print Culture: An Introduction." In *New Directions in Book History: The Perils of Print Culture: Book, Print and Publishing History in Theory and Practice*. Edited by Jason McElligott and Eve Patten, 1–16. London: Palgrave Macmillan, 2014.

McEwen, Gilbert D. *The Oracle of the Coffee House: John Dunton's Athenian Mercury*. San Marino, CA: The Huntington Library, 1972.

McGuiness, Rosamunde. "Musical Provocation in Eighteenth-Century London: The 'British Apollo.'" *Music and Letters* 68, no.4 (1987): 333–42.

McKitterick, David. *Print, Manuscript and the Search for Order 1450–1830*. Cambridge: Cambridge University Press, 2003.

McLeod, W., and V. *A Graphical Directory of English Newspapers and Periodicals, 1702– 1714*. West Virginia School of Journalism, 1982.

McTague, John. "'There Is No Such Man as Isaack Bickerstaff': Patridge, Pittis, and Jonathan Swift." *Eighteenth-Century Life* 35, no.1 (2011): 83–101.

*Mercurious Brianticus Alive Again* (1648).

*Mercurious Politicus* (1650).

*Mercurious Pragmaticus* (1648).

Miguel-Alfonso, Richardo. "Social Conservatism, Aesthetic Education, and the Essay Genre in Eliza Haywood's Female Spectator." In *Fair Philosopher: Eliza Haywood and the Female Spectator*. Edited by Lynn Marie Wright and Donald J. Newman, 31–40. Lewisburg, PA: Bucknell University Press, 2006.

Milburn, Joshua Fields, and Ryan Nicodemus. "How to Start a Successful Blog in 2023." July 5, 2023. www.theminimalists.com/blog/.

Milmo, Dan. "TikTok Is Fastest Growing News Source for UK Adults, Ofcom Finds." *The Guardian*. July 20, 2022. www.theguardian.com/technology/2022/jul/21/tiktok-is-fastest-growing-news-source-for-uk-adults-ofcom-finds.

Muddiman, J. G. *The King's Journalist, 1659–1689: Studies in the Reign of Charles II*. London: John Lane The Bodley Head, 1923.

Novak, Maximillian E. *Daniel Defoe: Master of Fictions*. Oxford: Oxford University Press, 2001.

Nussbaum, Felicity. "Actresses and the Economics of Celebrity, 1700–1800." In *Theatre and Celebrity in Britain 1660–2000*. Edited by Mary Luckhurst and Jane Moody, 148–68. London: Palgrave Macmillan, 2005.

Nussbaum, Felicity. *Rival Queens: Actresses, Performance, and the Eighteenth-Century British Theater*. Philadelphia, PA: University of Pennsylvania Press, 2011.

Osell, Tedra S. "The Ghost Writer: English Essay Periodicals and the Materialization of the Public in the Eighteenth Century." Dissertation: University of Washington, 2002.

Osell, Tedra. "Tatling Women in the Public Sphere: Rhetorical Femininity and the English Periodical Essay." *Eighteenth-Century Studies* 38, no.2 (2005): 283–300.

*Parrot*. London: 1728; 1746.

Parsons, Nicola. "The Ladies Mercury." In *Women's Periodicals and Print Culture*. Edited by Batchelor, Jennie and Manushag N. Powell, 315–27.

Parsons, Nicola. *Reading Gossip in Early Eighteenth-Century England*. London: Palgrave Macmillan, 2009. https://doi-org.srv-proxy1.library.tamu.edu/10.1057/9780230244764_5.

Penn, Sara. "The Female Spectator: The First Periodical by and for Women." *The Women's Print History Project*, February 25, 2021, https://womensprinthistoryproject.com/blog/post/63.

Peterson, Carla L. "Mapping Taste: Urban Modernities from the Tatler and Spectator to Frederick Douglass' Paper." *American Literary History* 32, no.4 (2020): 691–722.

Pettit, Alexander. "Adventures in Pornographic Paces: Eliza Haywood's Tea-Table and Decentering Moral Argument." *Papers on Language and Literature* 38 (2002): 244–69.

*Philosophical Transactions*. www.jstor.org/stable/101400.

*Poetical Courant*. London: Benjamin Bragg, 1706.

Poovey, Mary. "The Liberal Civil Subject and the Social in Eighteenth-Century British Moral Philosophy." *Public Culture* 14, no.1 (2002): 125–45.

Powell, Manushag N. "Johnson and His 'Readers' in the Epistolary Rambler Essays." *Studies in English Literature* 44, no.3 (2004): 573–94.

Powell, Manushag N. *Performing Authorship in Eighteenth-Century English Periodicals*. Lewisburg, PA: Bucknell Press, 2012.

Radice, Mark A. "Henry Purcell's Contributions to the Gentleman's Journal. *Bach* 9, no.4 (1978): 25–30.

Raymond, Joad. *Making the News: An Anthology of the Newsbooks of Revolutionary England 1641–1660*. London: St. Martin's Press, 1993.

Raymond, Joad. "The Daily Muse; or, Seventeenth-Century Poets Read the News." *The Seventeenth Century* 10 (2018): 189–218.

Raymond, Joad. *The Invention of the Newspaper: English Newsbooks 1641–1649*. Oxford: Oxford University Press, 2005.

*Reader*. London: Jacob Tonson, 1714.

*Records of Love: Or, Weekly Amusements for the Fair Sex*. London: J. Grantham, 1710.

Reed, Henry. *Lectures on English Literatures: From Chaucer to Tennyson*. 2nd ed. Philadelphia, PA: Parry and McMillan, 1855.

Richetti, John J. *The Life of Daniel Defoe: A Critical Biography.* London: Wiley-Blackwell, 2015.

Roach, Joseph. *It.* Ann Arbor, MI: University of Michigan Press, 2007.

Rogers, Pat. “Addison, Joseph (1672–1719), Writer and Politician.” *Oxford Dictionary of National Biography.* September 23, 2004; Accessed August 8, 2023.

Ross, Slaney Chadwick. “John Dunton’s Ladies Mercury and the Eighteenth-Century Female Subject.” In *Women’s Periodicals and Print Culture.* Edited by Batchelor, Jennie and Manushag N. Powell, Edinburgh: Edinburgh University Press, 2018, 327–41.

“The Royal Society of London Philosophical Transactions: 350 Years of Publishing at the Royal Society 1665–2015.” https://royalsociety.org/journals/publishing-activities/publishing350/history-philosophical-transactions/.

Schellenberg, Betty A. *Literary Coteries and the Making of Modern Print Culture 1740–1790.* Cambridge: Cambridge University Press, 2016.

Shevelow, Kathryn. “Re-Writing the Moral Essay: Eliza Haywood’s Female Spectator.” *Reader* 13 (1985): 19–31.

Shevelow, Kathryn. *Women and Print Culture: The Construction of Femininity in the Early Periodical.* London: Routledge, 1989.

Sievers, Julie. “Literatures of Wonder in Early Modern England and America.” *Literature Compass* 4, no.3 (2007):766–83. https://doi.org/10.1111/j.1741-4113.2007.00450.x.

Skains, R. Lyle. *Digital Authorship: Publishing in the Attention Economy.* Cambridge: Cambridge University Press, 2019.

Smith, John Harrington. “Thomas Baker and ‘The Female Tatler.’” *Modern Philology* 49, no. 3 (1952): 182–88.

Sommerville, C. John. *The News Revolution in England: Cultural Dynamic of Daily Information.* Oxford: Oxford University Press, 1996.

“The *Spectator.*” https://virginia-anthology.org/the-spectator/.

Spedding, Patrick. *A Bibliography of Eliza Haywood.* London: Pickering & Chatto, 2004.

Spufford, Margaret. “First Steps in Literacy: The Reading and Writing Experiences of the Humblest Seventeenth-Century Spiritual Autobiographers.” *Social History* 4 (1979): 407–35.

Steele, Richard. *The Tatler.* 3 Vols. Edited by Donald A. Bond. Oxford: Oxford University Press, 1987.

Sutherland, James. *The Restoration Newspaper and Its Development.* Cambridge: Cambridge University Press, 1986.

Temple, William. “To the Athenian Society.” In *The Athenian Mercury. Supplement to Volume Five.* London: John Dunton, 1691.

Tierney, James. "British Periodicals: Problems and Progress." *The Papers of the Bibliographical Society of America* 69, no.2 (1975): 165–86.

Todd, Todd. *William Dockwra and the Rest of the Undertakers: The Story of the London Penny Post*. London: C.J. Cousland, 1952.

Vázquez-Herrero, J., M. -C., Negreira-Rey, and X. López-García. "Let's Dance the News! How the News Media Are Adapting to the Logic of TikTok." *Journalism* 23 (2020): 1717–35. https://doi.org/10.1177/1464884920969092.

*Wentworth Papers 1705-1739*. Edited by James J. Cartwright. London: Wyman and Sons, 1883.

Wessel, Kristen. "Sound You Seek out Online Press or Print Placements?" *Forbes*, January 25, 2022. www.forbes.com/sites/forbescommunicationscouncil/2022/01/25/should-you-seek-out-online-press-or-print-placements/?sh=47ac43f47fb6.

White, Robert Benjamin. *A Study of the Female Tatler* (1709–1711). Ph.D Dissertation. University of North Carolina, 1966.

Wilkinson, Hazel. "The Complete Spectator: A Bibliographical History. In *Joseph Addison: Tercentenary Essays*. Edited by Paul Davis, 182–211. Oxford: Oxford University Press, 2021.

Williams, Abigail. *The Social Life of Books: Reading Together in the Eighteenth-Century Home*. New Haven: Yale University Press, 2017.

Williams, Bruce A., and Michael X. Delli Carpini. *After Broadcast News: Media, Regimes, Democracy, and the New Information Environment*. Cambridge: Cambridge University Press, 2011.

Williams, Bruce A. and Michael X. Delli Carpini. *And That's the Way It (Was): The Rise and Fall of the Age of Broadcast News*. Cambridge: Cambridge University Press, 2011, p. 59.

Winton, Calhoun. "Steele, Sir Richard (bap. 1672, d. 1729), Writer and Politician." *Oxford Dictionary of National Biography*. September 23, 2004; Accessed August 8, 2023.

Woudhuysen, Henry Ruxton. *Sir Philip Sidney and the Circulation of Manuscripts 1558–1640*. Oxford: Clarendon Press 1996.

Wright, Lynn Marie, and Donald J. Newman, eds. *Fair Philosopher: Eliza Haywood and the Female Spectator*. Lewisburg, PA: Bucknell Press, 2006.

# Acknowledgments

I am grateful to Texas A&M University and the John and Sara Lindsey Chair of Liberal Arts for supporting this research and its Open Access publication. I enjoyed the help and expertise of multiple libraries and librarians including the British Library, the Bodleian, and Cushing Memorial Library at A&M; Celine Luppo McDaid at Dr. Johnson's House, London, was particularly gracious in letting me explore that library and Aaron Pratt at the Harry Ransom Center, UT Austin, gave generously of his time and expertise. Early readers include Vera Camdem and Lawrence Griffing, and I had very helpful conversations about digital skeuomorphs with Alexander and Daniel Griffing. In particular I would like to recognize two very important "influencers" in my intellectual life, J. Paul Hunter at the start and Robert Hume towards the end. Finally, this Element would not have been possible without the insights and encouragement of Eve Tavor Bannet, who didn't think it odd to discuss Aphra Behn and Japanese cell phone novels in the same conversation.

## Cambridge Elements

# Eighteenth-Century Connections



## About the Series

Exploring connections between verbal and visual texts and the people, networks, cultures and places that engendered and enjoyed them during the long Eighteenth Century, this innovative series also examines the period's uses of oral, written and visual media, and experiments with the digital platform to facilitate communication of original scholarship with both colleagues and students.

Cambridge Elements

# Eighteenth-Century Connections

## Elements in the Series

*Voltaire's Correspondence: Digital Readings*
Nicholas Cronk and Glenn Roe

*Mary Prince, Slavery, and Print Culture in the Anglophone Atlantic World*
Juliet Shields

*Disavowing Disability: Richard Baxter and the Conditions of Salvation*
Andrew McKendry

*How and Why to Do Things with Eighteenth-Century Manuscripts*
Michelle Levy and Betty A. Schellenberg

*Philosophical Connections: Akenside, Neoclassicism, Romanticism*
Chris Townsend

*Empirical Knowledge in the Eighteenth-Century Novel: Beyond Realism*
Aaron R. Hanlon

*Secret Writing in the Long Eighteenth Century: Theories and Practices of Cryptology*
Katherine Ellison

*Science and Reading in the Eighteenth Century: The Hardwicke Circle and the Royal Society, 1740–1766*
Markman Ellis

*Early English Periodicals and Early Modern Social Media*
Margaret J. M. Ezell

A full series listing is available at: www.cambridge.org/EECC

For EU product safety concerns, contact us at Calle de José Abascal, 56–1°,
28003 Madrid, Spain or eugpsr@cambridge.org.

www.ingramcontent.com/pod-product-compliance
Ingram Content Group UK Ltd.
Pitfield, Milton Keynes, MK11 3LW, UK
UKHW022146080726
473066UK00010B/801
* 9 7 8 1 1 0 8 7 9 1 7 4 8 *